RICHARD N. S. WALMSLEY

THE BRI

Ahead

Other Books by Richard Andersen

POWER WRITE: A PRACTICAL GUIDE TO WORDS THAT WORK
THE WRITE STUFF: A PRACTICAL GUIDE TO STYLE AND MECHANICS
WRITE IT RIGHT: A GUIDE TO CLEAR AND CORRECT WRITING
WRITING THAT WORKS: A PRACTICAL GUIDE FOR BUSINESS AND CREATIVE PEOPLE

Getting Ahead

Career Skills That Work for Everyone

Richard Andersen

McGraw-Hill, Inc.

New York   San Francisco   Washington, D.C.   Auckland   Bogotá
Caracas   Lisbon   London   Madrid   Mexico City   Milan
Montreal   New Delhi   San Juan   Singapore
Sydney   Tokyo   Toronto

Library of Congress Cataloging-in-Publication Data

Andersen, Richard   [Date]
  Getting ahead : career skills that work for everyone / Richard Andersen.

      p.   cm.
  Includes index.
  ISBN 0-07-001765-4 (acid-free paper).– ISBN 0-07-001766-2 (pbk.)
  1. Job hunting.   2. Career development.   3. Business communication.
4. Interpersonal communication.   5. Success in business.   6. Job
satisfaction.   I. Title.
HF5382.7.A55   1995
650.14–dc20   94-31601
                                                          CIP

1 2 3 4 5 6 7 8 9 0   DOC/DOC   9 0 9 8 7 6 5 4   (hc)
1 2 3 4 5 6 7 8 9 0   DOC/DOC   9 0 9 8 7 6 5 4   (pbk)

ISBN 0-07-001766-2 (pbk)
ISBN 0-07-001765-4 (hc)

*The sponsoring editor for this book was Betsy N. Brown, the editing
supervisor was Fred Dahl, and the production supervisor was Donald
Schmidt. It was set in Baskerville by Inkwell Publishing Services.*

Printed and bound by R. R. Donnelley & Sons Company.

For Eleni,
who stays ahead and keeps us whole

Contents

How to Use This Book   xii

Part 1. Laying the Foundation for Success

1. **How to Develop the Right Attitude**   **3**
   The Right Attitude   4
   Right Action   7

2. **How to Make Changes in Your Life**   **9**

3. **How to Set Goals You Can Reach**   **11**
   Goals   11
   Action Plan   12

4. **How to Get Organized**   **16**

5. **How to Stop Procrastinating**   **19**

6. **How to Manage Your Time Better**   **22**

7. **How to Take Control of Your Projects**   **32**
   Plan   32
   Act   34
   Review   35

8. **How to Use Words That Work**   **36**

Part 2. Getting the Job You Want

9. How to Create an Eye-Catching Resume   **43**
Some Final Thoughts on Resumes   49

10. How to Write a Cover Letter That Gets Read   **50**

11. How to Make Every Interview a Success   **54**
Before Your Interview   55
During Your Interview   57
After the Interview   60

Part 3. Developing Your Personal Communication Skills

12. How to Improve Your Writing Skills   **63**
Think   63
Write   65
Correct   65

13. How to Write Better Memos and Letters   **68**
A Format for Memos   70
A Format for Letters   70
Before Writing Any Memo or Letter Ask Yourself   71
A Final Word About Writing   73

14. How to Read Faster and Remember More   **74**
To Read Faster   74
To Remember More   77
Two Important Things to Remember About Remembering   79

15. How to Listen to What You Hear   **81**
To Hear and Select   81
To Determine   83
To Reply   84

16. How to Do Business over the Phone   **86**
For the Calls We Take   86
For the Calls We Make   86
And Now for the Tough Calls   97

17. How to Create Effective Presentations   **94**
Any Questions?   99

18. How to Make Every Meeting Worthwhile   101

19. How to Negotiate Win-Win Situations   106

Part 4. Managing Yourself

20. How to Manage Stress   113

21. How to Assert Yourself   119

22. How to Combat Job Burnout   124

23. How to Be More Creative   127

24. How to Take Risks   130

25. How to Handle Sexual Harassment   133

26. How to Have a Family and a Career   135
   Arranging Child Care at Home   136
   Arranging Child Care at a Center   137
   Getting Help Around the House   138
   Creating Time   139
   Combating Guilt   139

Part 5. Leading Others

27. How to Supervise   143

28. How to Deal with Difficult People   148
   Directors   148
   Relators   149
   Thinkers   150
   Operators   150

29. How to Manage Conflict   153
   Preparing for Conflict   153
   Using the Conflict   154
   Monitoring the Agreement   155
   A Final Note on Conflict Resolution   156

30. How to Delegate   157

31. How to Give and Take Criticism   **162**

How to Respond to Criticism   163
If You Must Be Negative, Do It Positively   165
A Final Note on Giving Criticism   167

32. How to Motivate Others   **169**

An Alternative to Maslow   173
Affiliation   173
Power   173
Achievement   174

33. How to Conduct Win-Win Reviews   **175**

Before the Appraisal Meeting   175
What to Do If You're the One Being Reviewed   177

34. How to Hire and Fire   **179**

How to Hire   179
How to Fire   181

35. How to Create Self-Managed Work Teams   **183**

Stage 1: Unconscious Incompetence   186
Stage 2: Conscious Incompetence   186
Stage 3: Conscious Competence   189
Stage 4: Unconscious Competence   193
A Final Word on Teams   195

Index   197

How to Use
This Book

Ten minutes before I came up with the idea to write this book, I was talking with my friend John Tichenor. John is Fax International's top sales representative. And John was telling me how he has all these books on how to be more effective at what he does. Everything from *You Can Sell* to Stephen Covey's book on habits. "You name it; I got it."

And he has them everywhere. At his desk at work, on his desk in the basement of his home, by his chair in the den, on his night table upstairs, in the bathrooms (all three and one-half), even next to the televisions ("for the commercials").

Only John doesn't read any of his books. Or much of any of them. "I start but, before I can get to the point of any chapter, I have to go do something. That's the trouble with books. They're all written by writers. If they had to work real jobs, they wouldn't have the time to fill up so many pages between the points they make. And because I never have the time to get to wherever these writers are supposed to be taking me, I never remember anything I read. I need an *All I Ever Needed to Know I Learned in Kindergarten* for business people."

John, your wish has just been granted.

Getting Ahead: Career Skills That Work for Everyone is not to be read. At least not from cover to cover. It's for looking up information. Quick, easy-to-read, practical information that gets right to the point about what you need to know to perform better at whatever you do.

Here's how it works. Say you're going to a review meeting where your boss will evaluate your performance for the past six months. But your boss is the kind who conducts reviews with sentences like, "We're really proud of the way you handled the FSC problem, and you did a great job containing the damage with Johnson, but . . . ."

That *but* seems to negate everything that came before it, and now you have to listen to yourself being trashed for the next half hour.

This book will help you get your boss to focus more on what you did right. It will also tell you how to turn your boss's negatives into positives. In his or her eyes as well as your own. (If you're already a boss, this book will help you improve your workers' performance without making them feel diminished.)

What you want to do is this: The day before you go into your next review meeting, look up the chapters on negotiation and reviews (your perspective and your boss's). You'll notice that these chapters, like all the other chapters in *Getting Ahead*, are short. There's little theorizing, few case histories, and lots of white space on each page to help you read more easily. You probably won't want to follow all the suggestions in any given chapter. Not every piece of advice will apply to every reader or to every job. So you take what you need, use it, and forget about the rest until your next review.

Getting Ahead can't guarantee that you'll get every job, win every negotiation, or satisfy every customer, but it will help you compete more effectively for every job, win something in every negotiation, and satisfy more customers in more ways than ever before. And once *Getting Ahead* helps get you to the top in your company or field, it provides you with the new skills you'll need to meet the new challenges that await you.

Enough said and enough read. The next time you need a readily adaptable solution to the kind of problems you face almost daily in business and industry, you know where to find it.

Well, my time is just about up. If you have any other questions about public speaking or anything else in this book, write to me:

Richard Andersen
c/o McGraw-Hill, Inc.

Betsy Brown is the book's editor (did she do a great job or what?), and we're both eager to read and reply to anything you send us.

RICHARD ANDERSEN
Amherst, Massachusetts

Getting Ahead

Part 1
Laying the Foundation for Success

Personal responsibility is our greatest
evolution. The idea that we are all products of
our environment is our greatest sin.
                              MARGARET MEAD

1

How to Develop the Right Attitude

So much has been written and spoken about self-esteem that its become the all-purpose excuse for failure. If only you had higher self-esteem, you would be happier in your personal relationships and more successful in your career.

Nonsense!

Trying to build your self-esteem before you attempt to make a change in your personal or professional life is like trying to swim without going in the water. Work instead on improving your attitude and skills (behavioral as well as technical), achieve some success in whatever direction you want to head in, and a healthy dose of self-esteem will not be far behind. In other words, nothing increases self-esteem like success.

Think, for example, of any book or tape on self-esteem that you ever read or listened to. How did it begin? Probably with a quiz designed to show you how insecure you are:

- Do you ever ask yourself why you're not more successful?
- Are you ever afraid of looking foolish in front of others?
- Do you tend to avoid people you don't like?
- Could your attitude toward your life improve?
- Do you ever blame others for the things that have gone wrong in your life?

If you didn't answer "yes" to all of these questions, you wouldn't be normal. Yet these questions and dozens like them are used to manipulate you into thinking less of yourself. Then, when the authors and speakers of these books and tapes have you on the canvas of their ring, they provide tips to help you get back on your feet.

That kind of help you don't need.

Focus instead on repeating what already works, correcting what doesn't, and learning new ways to improve. With each success that follows — personal or professional — you will build the confidence you need to feel good about yourself and meet the increasingly difficult challenges of the future.

Each of the following chapters in this book provides behavioral and technical advice on how to be better at whatever you want to do, but none of these suggestions will work if you don't meld them with:

The Right Attitude

Without the Right Attitude, you can apply all the techniques you want and never come off as being more than a phony, a fool, and a failure.

So how do you develop the Right Attitude necessary to make your new-found skills work?

Be yourself. Do not be someone else's idea of who you should be, including husbands, wives, relatives, and friends as well as bosses, colleagues, and clients. Trying to conform to the images others create for you is to become mentally anoretic. While you shrink into a mere skeleton of what you could be, all you can see is the psychological fat you've been trained to attack yourself with.

Forget about the past. Erase the part of your past that can undermine you now. Repeat what worked, learn from your mistakes, and throw out whatever emotional baggage is keeping you from advancement.

If, for reasons other than success, you want to understand your past history, the fastest and most effective way is to change your behavior. Then compare the differences brought about by the changes.

Imagine the ideal you. "You" is the key word here, not someone else's idea of who you should be. In other words, stop "shoulding" on yourself. Instead, create a mental picture of yourself that includes not only your best qualities but the level of achievement you want these qualities to help you reach.

Think, look, and act the part. If your image of yourself is to be a successful sales representative, think of yourself as already being a successful sales representative. You may not be the best salesperson in the company (there can only be one of those), but you can be one of the best. So think of yourself as already being one of the best.

Now ask yourself, "How does one of the best dress and behave in the presence of clients, colleagues, customers, and supervisors?" Got the picture? Good. Now stop thinking and start acting. Follow in your behavior the blueprint you created in your mind.

Don't compare yourself with others. Whether you win or lose, the process is a waste of time. Everybody's different, and everybody has something to contribute. Focus instead on what you do well, discover how you can do it better, and work on how you can improve in areas where your performance isn't what you think it should be.

Don't let anybody drag you down. If someone is rude, inconsiderate, or aggressive, don't take their behavior personally. Tell yourself, "It's them; it's not me." Then ask yourself if you can change the way you behave toward these people. If they can see you differently, they might act differently toward you.

Compliment them. Ask them about the subjects in the photographs on their desks. Talk about what they like to talk about. We live in an age of increasing dehumanization. In times of increasing dehumanization, people look for human contact. Those of us who provide human contact will develop better relationships. Think of the people you like to talk to on the phone at work. Do you want to spend time with the people who state their business and disconnect, or do you want to hear from the people who bring a little more to their conversation than just business? The same is true for the people who deal with you.

Think, then, of each rude remark as a cry for help. Or at least attention. Realize that the people who made these remarks are probably in some kind of pain. And they probably wouldn't say what they did if they didn't trust you not to hold their offensive behavior against them.

To get along better with these people, look beneath the surface of their words to the psychological drama that is taking place underneath. Respond to the issues they raise but be sensitive to the drama. *Take responsibility for your actions.* Accept the fact that you're going to make mistakes and admit your share of the responsibility when you do. Don't waste time looking for excuses and don't undermine yourself by blaming others. Once you start pointing a finger at someone else, you turn yourself into a victim. And victims are losers. The only thing they can ever win for themselves is pity. Yet, they can wreak havoc on you. Victims rationalize everything that doesn't go their way, are always right, make others feel guilty for not being victims, look to winners to rescue them, and then resent and eventually punish their rescuers for having the power victims lack, namely, the ability to conquer their fears, overcome their anxieties, and manage their lives.

Reward your accomplishments. Regardless of how small they may be, take note of your accomplishments. Psychologists have discovered that lack of closure and celebration is one of the most common causes of stress in the American workplace. So take the time to enjoy what you've done. Treat yourself to a dinner, a movie or, if you can, some time off from work. Start making a mental accomplishment list at the end of each day. Include anything you were able to achieve since you woke up that morning. For some people, just getting out of bed is a major accomplishment.

Make the best use of your free time. Your education, intelligence, and levels of social awareness can all be measured by how you spend your free time. This doesn't mean, however, that everything you do should add up to some tangible betterment of yourself. Bertrand Russell once said, "The time we enjoy wasting is not wasted time."

Don't be afraid. Fear is not a sign of failure; it is a sign of fear. It's not a behavior; it's an emotion, so don't fight it. Instead, go with it. A little fear can take you a long way toward helping you succeed. If you're afraid, you probably have some good reasons to be afraid. So ask yourself: "What's the worst that could possibly happen?" If that worst thing happened, what would you do? Since the worst thing probably won't happen, how would you handle the next worst thing? Instead of looking at any disaster from your present point of view, look at it as if it has already taken place. By starting with the worst outcome and working backwards, you can anticipate these disasters and make plans to avoid them. In other words, your solutions make up an important part of your blueprint for success, and each solution is another rung down the ladder of fear.

Being successful doesn't mean you have no fear, never get nervous, or occasionally think you won't win. Being successful means having the confidence to accept who you are while working to make yourself better. Your fears will subside in proportion to the success you achieve.

Your attitude is the lens through which you view your world. How you choose to frame the experiences of your life is up to you. If you choose to see a glass that is half full of water rather than one that is half empty, you will. It's as simple and as complex as that.

Having the right attitude toward yourself and your work doesn't guarantee success, but having the wrong attitude almost certainly guarantees failure. Or at best, stagnation. If you think you won't get the job, the promotion or the raise, you probably won't. And if you do, you'll credit luck, or another person's mistakes, or something else outside of your control. Not only will you prevent yourself from developing the kind of confidence you need to succeed, you'll see yourself as an imposter for whom it will only be a matter of time before your shortcomings are revealed and you fail. And you know what? You'll be right!

But having the Right Attitude is not enough. Right Attitude has to be combined with:

Right Action

Right Action People vs.	*Wrong Action People*
Take fate into their own hands. They plan and act in the present to prevent crises in the future. They know that luck is the residue of design and hard work.	Allow circumstances to dictate their behavior. That way they always have an excuse for why they fail.
Are quality driven. They bring to their tasks a sense of vision and integrity. It's not just what they do; it's how they do it and how they make you feel when it's done.	Don't do anything that isn't in their job description. That way they never have to take a risk or be responsible for anything other than what they were hired to do.
Concentrate on what they can control and allow word of their accomplishments to expand their spheres of influence.	Create anxiety for themselves and others by frequently worrying about what they can't do anything about.
Do things right. They take risks to satisfy the needs of customers, clients, and colleagues.	Do what's right. They play by the book, follow the rules, and make no exceptions for anyone.

To become Right Active:

Ask what you can change in your life. Then determine how you can make that change and how long it will take you to complete that change.

Focus on what you can control. Worrying about what's outside of your control will only lead to frustration, disappointment, and failure.

Be willing to take risks. Sometimes you will fail, but success isn't possible without risk.

Be patient. You can't overcome all your bad habits in the time it takes you to plan what you want to change in your life. But you can start to overcome those bad habits in the time it takes you to create that plan.

Repeat what works for others as well as yourself. What did others in your company or field do to be successful? Your answer provides an example for you to follow.

Do it all over again. Being Right Active isn't a one-time thing; it's a life-long process of self-renewal. The old Wrong-Active attitude is: "If it ain't broke, don't fix it." The new Right-Active position is: "If it ain't broke, you haven't looked hard enough."

Right Attitude is a state of mind; Right Action is a state of being. It measures your commitment to what you believe in. In other words, there are a lot of people walking around with the Right Attitude, but their Right Attitude doesn't always translate into Right Action. The major reason for this can be summed up in three words: Fear of change.

2
How to Make Changes in Your Life

Most people fear change. Set in their ways, they equate it with destruction. And they're right. Something old has to be destroyed for something new to take its place. Letting go of the familiar and adjusting to the not yet known is a difficult transition. And that difficulty is made worse by the number of times people are now expected to make changes in their lives.

How do people respond to changes? The few who are on the cutting edge, effecting new directions and benefiting from them, like change. Another percentage of the population refuses to change. These people pick a time warp in their lives and live there. The great majority of people are uncomfortable with change but go along with it because they have no other choice. If they don't change, they will become dinosaurs.

To learn to live in a world that is constantly changing:

Chuck the obsolete. If it's no longer effective, get rid of it. Look for your door of opportunity in the new. Imagine how the new will benefit you. How it will increase your behavioral and technical skills, make your more competitive, help you build stronger relationships with the people who are important to you.

Keep an open mind. We don't want to blindly accept the new just because it's new, but neither do we want to reject the new because it's different. Think of the new as neither good nor bad but something that should be given a chance to be judged on its own merits.

Take action. Instead of thinking, "This is happening to me," think "This is what I can do with the new." If what you try to do with the new doesn't work, try something else. Look for as many possibilities as you can, and "It won't work" will rarely be your conclusion.

Be patient. Give the new a chance to work. Studies have shown that it takes an average of 21 days to successfully break a habit and begin to form a new one.

Be flexible. Don't get stuck in the old, and don't get stuck in the new that doesn't work. Experiment. Discover what you can learn from any failed solution; today's failure is often tomorrow's opportunity for success.

Ask for help. You're new at the new and the information you need to succeed may not yet be found in books, so ask. Even if you don't get a solution, you'll discover something to think about, something that may lead to the solution you're looking for.

Don't give up. Setbacks aren't failures; they're setbacks. Think of them as beginnings not ends.

Accentuate the positive. If negative thinking can create a self-fulfilling prophecy, so can positive thinking. Recognize your strengths, strengthen your weaknesses, and celebrate your accomplishments.

Maintain a sense of humor. Don't take yourself too seriously. Samuel Beckett once said, "There is no situation in life that can't be overcome with laughter."

Visualize a successful outcome. This will help you break away from any past habits that encourage you to resist change, it will make aware of more opportunities than you had given the new credit for, and it will serve as your guide as you make your transition from the old.

3

How to Set Goals You Can Reach

We all have wants and needs. Unfortunately, these wants and needs often remain just that: wants and needs. To make your wants and needs a reality, you need to turn them into. . .

Goals

Your goals may be personal (e.g., a better relationship with your spouse) or professional (e.g., a promotion that gives you more control in your company) or both (e.g., a job that gets you away from your computer and working with people). These goals define the life you want for yourself, the end product toward which you want to direct most of your energy.

Some goals are easier to attain than others, but your chances of achieving your goals are increased if they contain these five characteristics:

S: *Specific.* "To write a proposal" is not a goal; it's just a want or a need. "To write three pages daily until the project is completed" is a specific goal. "To have more free time" is a dream. "To have three weeks to travel to Greece" is a goal. Another advantage of a specific goal: you know when you've reached it.

M: *Measurable.* Measuring your progress toward any goal helps you keep you on track. Every measurement tells you how far you've come and how far you have to go.

A: *Attainable.* Given your available resources (time, money, education, experience, and skills), is your goal possible to achieve within a reasonable amount of time, say no more than five years? Try not to aim either too high or too low; both weaken motivation.

R: *Realistic.* Are your goals what you really want? If more money is your goal, what in your present life will you be willing to sacrifice to help you reach that goal? Maybe the money you want to make isn't worth the time you'd have to take away from being with your family. Maybe the power you'd get with a promotion wouldn't be worth the added responsibilities you'd have to take on.

T: *Time.* Deadlines, when used effectively, have been shown to increase productivity and quality. The key to reaching the deadline you set for the attainment of any goal is to have a series of minideadlines leading up to your final deadline. In other words, if you plan to reach a certain goal by the last day of next month, your chances of meeting that deadline are increased if you divide your work into a series of tasks, each one to be completed by a specific date between now and your final deadline. You may wish, for example, to have so much work done by the first of next month, so much by the tenth, and so much more by the twentieth. Establishing an ultimate deadline puts pressure on you to work; establishing minideadlines spreads that pressure out and allows you to focus on one task at a time.

To determine what goals are SMART for you, make a list of all your wants and needs, personal and professional. Don't hold anything back. No matter how wild your dream might be, write it down. Once all your visions of the life you want are on paper, eliminate the ones that don't meet the SMART criteria. If you're like most people, you won't have more than five.

Now record each goal on a separate piece of paper. Listing each goal separately will make your goal more real for you, and it will be easier to achieve than if you carry it around in your head. In you head, your goal can be replaced by more immediate concerns; on paper, your goal is a constant reminder as to where you should be directing your energy and a continual measurement as to how much progress you've made.

With each goal now recorded on a separate piece of paper, your next step is to create an. . .

Action Plan

Your Action Plan is the steps you need to take to reach any single goal. Start with the goal that's most important to you. Ask yourself, "What do I need to do to reach this goal?" List your answers in whatever order they come to mind. Once your answers are on the page and you can see them all at once, order your answers into a list of priorities. Start with the one that is easiest to achieve, that you can begin work on the soonest and that will enable you to quickly reach a first level of accomplishment. As you reach each level of accomplishment, you will gain the confidence you need to succeed at the next level.

Here are some things to do to help you create an effective Action Plan:

Visualize. Imagine yourself already having achieved your goal. How do you feel? How has your life changed? What advantages have come to you since your goal was reached?

Now ask yourself: What did I have to do to reach this goal? Your answers will be important steps to follow in your Action Plan.

Talk. Let anyone who can help you reach your goal know what you plan to do. If they've achieved a similar goal, they may have some suggestions.

Identify problems. Include everything from daily interruptions and distractions to long-held fears and bad habits. What can you do about them? Start with the easiest first.

In the chapter on Right Attitude, we talked about fear of failure, but what about fear of success? That can be a barrier too. Ask yourself:

- Will I no longer be attractive to some people once I'm successful?
- Will I be blamed when someone under my supervision makes a mistake?
- What if I'm really only fulfilling my parent's or spouse's ambitions and not my own?
- What if I feel I don't really deserve to be successful?

Fortunately, the techniques for handling fear of failure also apply to fear of success. Imagine yourself in the worst possible situation. Make a list of all the consequences you fear. Then visualize how you would handle each of these consequences. What will you say and how will you behave, for example, when a supervisor holds you responsible for someone else's failure? The more responses you can come up with, the more ways you'll think of to prevent that failure and, with those ways, your fears will be alleviated.

To implement your Action Plan:

Keep focused. More often than not, the immediate satisfaction that comes from participating in an activity that distracts you from your Action

Plan is not going to be as rewarding as one that helps you reach your goal.

Be flexible. Being flexible and staying focused are not contradictions in terms. Your goals are written on a piece of paper; they're not carved in stone. As you come closer to achieving your goal, you may decide it's not exactly what you want. Something you've discovered along the way now seems more attractive. How many people do you know who decided on a major their first year in college and wound up in a job they had only a secondary interest in? This is one reason why it's so important for us to know ourselves, but how many of us know ourselves so well as to know what we really want?

Do the next best thing: Establish what you think are the best goals for you, create the most effective Action Plan you can, and stay focused but be open to changes that might encourage you to reevaluate your goal. Change may be a threat but, more often than not, it's an opportunity.

Celebrate. Deadlines and hard work are important, but so is joy. Provide time in your Action Plan to appreciate your growth and celebrate your accomplishments. Your happiness, after all, should be one of the reasons you chose the goals.

To ensure the success of your Action Plan:

Get motivated. Desire is the link that connects your plans with your behavior. It's the driving force behind every step of your Action Plan and an important key to your success.

To get and stay motivated:

Accentuate the positive. Remind yourself of your past achievements and what you overcame to reach them. Take pride in your accomplishments. Recognize the fact that you deserve to get what you choose to work for.

Get a payoff. You'll do better work if there's something in your work for you. It doesn't have to be money; it can be status, respectability, appreciation, the satisfaction of completing a task, self-respect, praise, the people you work with, the difference you make in the lives of others, the fact that you're needed, that the office just wouldn't be the same without you. No job offers all the payoffs you may want; what's important is to have some of those things that matter most. The next most important thing is to do what you need to do to enjoy those payoffs.

Keep the end in mind. Visualize the rewards that you will reap once you reach your goal, think about how good you will feel when those rewards become a reality, and keep that picture and those rewards in mind to help you propel yourself to the new you.

Discipline means doing what you know has to be done even when you don't feel like doing it. It means sacrificing the now for the later, the easy for the hard, and the want for the must. To develop the discipline you need to succeed:

Be responsible. Discipline has very little to do with brains or talent, yet brains and talent are almost helpless without it. So be responsible to your goal and to yourself. The more disciplined you are, the more power and control you have over what you do. The more power and control you have, the better your chances of achieving success and ensuring your happiness.

Focus on the now. What can you do in the next five minutes to help you accomplish the first task on your Action Plan? So what if it's the easiest one! The tough ones aren't going anywhere. And the confidence you gain from completing the easier tasks will make the tougher ones less intimidating once you're ready to tackle them.

Get started. This last point cannot be overemphasized. The longer you wait to act, the harder it will be to begin. Start small and start now to develop the habits you'll need to overcome the more daunting tasks later on.

4

How to Get Organized

You weren't born organized and, since you've chosen to read this chapter, you probably know something about the mistakes, delays, and other setbacks that can come from being disorganized. Not to mention the frustration and anxiety a lack of effective organization can cause. Being organized, on the other hand, enables you to complete your tasks faster, easier, and more effectively. Not only do you have more control over your life, you also create more free time in it.

Although the single organizing system that satisfies every need is yet to be invented, there are some basic principles that all good organizing systems share:

Lists. One of the most proven and certainly the most common organizing method is the list. Lists of what you have to do remind you of what's important, enable you to prioritize your tasks, determine when and for how long you need to work on those tasks, and provide you with a sense of accomplishment as you check off each completed item.

The best time to make a list is either at the beginning or end of each day. And try not to think of your day as divided into exclusive sections: home, work, store, and so on. There's no reason why you can't run an errand during your lunch break, read a work-related document while waiting for a dental appointment, or plan a meeting agenda at home in the evening when you're relaxed and free from the distractions at work.

Goals (see pp. 11-12). Don't lose sight of them. Goals keep you heading in the right direction and focused on what's important, but they shouldn't be a tyrant. Accept the fact that some days just aren't long enough to complete every task you assign yourself. Anything that can't be done in one day should be moved to the next day and prioritized on you list.

Plans (see pp. 12-15). You can't juggle everything at once and not expect to drop something. So start small (one step at a time), start soon (the sooner the better), and be flexible (priorities change).

Calendars. Calendars keep track of your appointments and deadlines. Use only one (so you won't forget to transfer information), write in pencil (so you can change priorities), and check it daily (so you won't be surprised).

Rewards. Even if it's only to experience the satisfaction of crossing a completed item off you list, enjoy your accomplishments.

Organizing a life is one thing; organizing a work area is another. To organize your work area, divide (desk, bookcase, file cabinets) and conquer (whatever is furthest away from where you spend most of your time is the easiest to dispose of).

Your method of attack for each target is the same: reduce and rearrange.

Start with your bookcase. To reduce: Throw out duplicate copies, outdated catalogues, forgotten texts, journals you've never gotten around to reading, and anything you haven't used in a reasonable amount of time. To rearrange: Create broad categories of similar things. You may, for example, want to divide your bookcase into sections containing books, reference manuals, and reports in binders. It depends on the kind of work you do. Whatever method you choose, alphabetically arrange the works in each category.

Move on to the filing cabinet. To reduce: Throw out any files you no longer useor move into a storage area away from your work space. Eliminate dated, duplicate, and no longer relevant information from the files you do use. To rearrange: Consolidate your files into the broadest possible categories (big files are easier to handle than little ones); then consider ordering your files by how frequently you use them. Your most frequently-used files, for instance, could go in the drawer that's easiest for you to reach or in front of your less frequently used files. Alphabetize your labels within each category and consider identifying your categories with colored folders or colored tabs.

Finish with your desk. To reduce and rearrange: Dump or recycle whatever you don't frequently use. This includes everything from the broken equipment you never got around to fixing to the dried-out thinner you've held on to because you could never be sure when you might need it. Pens and pencils are important, but do you need a dozen of each? And what about that stapler and tape dispenser? Could they go in a drawer and free up some more workspace on the top of your desk? Limit the top of your desk to what you frequently use and what you're presently working on.

To keep your desk from piling up with things you don't need: Throw away whatever you can whenever you can, decide quickly what you want to do about whatever lands on your desk, complete each task as soon as possible, replace each file in your cabinet as soon as you're through using it, be selective about what you want to handle later, avoid writing notes on little pieces of paper (act on them right away or put all your notes in one notebook), and, at the end of each day, clear your desk of everything except what you plan to work on the following day.

Don't postpone organizing. Whether it's your desk or your life, being organized is better than being disorganized. And don't worry about losing your spontaneity, coming off as neurotic, or turning into a robot. Being organized gives you the peace of mind that enables you to be spontaneous and provides you with the free time to develop further your relationships with people. In short, it gives you the control you need to do what you want.

5

How to Stop Procrastinating

Procrastination — that special art of keeping up with yesterday — is not just a bad habit that thwarts progress and raises stress levels. For some, procrastination is a profound psychological illness that results in frustration, anger, and despair. If you've suffered setbacks as a result of procrastination but think it is no big deal and you can break your habit anytime you decide you really want to, this book won't help you. If, on the other hand, you've struggled with the pain of putting things off until the last minute and would like to learn some less anxiety-ridden ways of completing your tasks, read on.

Although there is only one major reason why people procrastinate (i.e., fear of failure), procrastinators have many excuses for what they don't do: the job is boring, the job is overwhelming, the conditions aren't conducive to work, the people overseeing the project are jerks, the deadlines are unreasonable, and so on.

To avoid procrastination:

Accept the fact that you procrastinate. But decide now to do something about it: grab a pencil, underline the suggestions in this book that best apply to you, copy those suggestions onto a separate piece of paper, and place that paper where you can't avoid seeing it.

List the things you can do right away. Start with the tasks that are easiest to complete and can be done in the shortest amount of time.

Live for five minutes at a time. Promise yourself to work non stop for five minutes on a project you've been postponing. Set an alarm clock to go off in five minutes; then start working as soon as the first second of your five minutes ticks. When the alarm clock goes off, stop, take a break (a deep breath, a sip of coffee), and admire what you were able to accomplish in just five minutes. Then repeat the process until you no longer need the clock.

Practice the Salami Technique. The Salami Technique is based on the theory that you would never eat a whole salami in one sitting. If you did, you'd wish you hadn't. The best way to eat a salami is to cut it up into small bite-sized pieces.

Same thing for any project that overwhelms you. Cut the project up into smaller segments and make a list of those segments. Then cut the first segment into a series of steps with each step able to be completed in a single working session.

Every time you start a new step, finish it before you leave your work area. Or stop your work at a place where it will be easy for you to start again when you return.

Whether you complete your step or break it off at a place where you can continue later, reward yourself for the work you accomplished.

Talk to others. Let the people who might be interested know what project you're working on and when you will finish it. Note the word "will." When talking about projects, avoid using words such as "try," "hope," and "should." What these words mean is that you don't want anyone to be upset with you when you fail. Also, talking to others about your project will increase your deadline pressure and give you the opportunity to seek advice.

List dates on your calendar. List all of them: the day you start, the day you will finish, and the dates of all the minideadlines in between. Again, the Salami Technique: A series of self-imposed minideadlines takes away some of the pressure of the final deadline, yet they maintain enough pressure to keep you heading toward your goal.

Stay awake. Procrastinators are almost always tired. You think it's easy to work at not getting any work done? It's exhausting. No matter how many tasks procrastinators begin and never finish, no matter how many things they do to avoid what they should do, the pressure to complete their most important project never ceases. In fact, it gets worse as the deadline approaches.

At the same time, these almost chronically fatigued procrastinators can work out in a gym or hang out in a bar or go shopping at a mall for hours and never show any signs of being tired. And do they feel great when they get out of the office! How many of them have you heard say, "Gee, I wish I didn't have to go to work tomorrow"? Nothing there but more pressure to blow off in a gym, bar, or mall.

To overcome procrastination fatigue, find something meaningful in your work, something you can believe in or some reason for doing it in a certain way or, if necessary, how good you will feel when the task is completed. Without a sense of purpose, your task will be either overwhelming or boring.

Strive for excellence rather than perfection. The worst procrastinators are perfectionists in disguise. Perfectionists have such high levels of expectation and such a low tolerance for criticism they become paralyzed. Nothing they do is good enough, and any criticism is an emotional earthquake.

Perfectionists don't delegate (no one can do it as well as they), don't ask for help (they know they're better than everyone else), resist any advice that is offered (they don't need someone to tell them what they already know). Perfectionists extend deadlines indefinitely (they need more time to make it good enough), and ignore the needs of others (as long as they're working, they're not finishing; as long as they're not finishing, they're avoiding criticism).

Excellent researchers, analysts, assessors, and compilers of information, this special breed of procrastinator takes great pride in being a perfectionist. It often gives them an air of arrogance that is not in any way undermined by the fact that they can't get anything done.

Perfectionists also have a long history of seeing their behavior rewarded. The perfectionists in school were very often those brilliant students who began their term papers the night before they were due. Because they were perfectionists, they always waited until the last minute to protect themselves from criticism but, because they knew the material so well, they always got high grades. If their teachers happened to find an error, the perfectionists told themselves that, had they not waited until the last moment, the paper would have been perfect.

Perfectionists, listen! It's not necessary to be perfect, just excellent (this advice is without further explanation because no perfectionist has read this far in this chapter).

Procrastinators, do your work. There's no guarantee that you won't meet with criticism but, if you don't do your work, failure is inevitable. If your best isn't good enough, learn from your mistakes. Learn also from what you did right. Anyone who has ever succeeded in anything has made mistakes, but even those who have strived for success and come up short are happier and feel more accomplished than those who never finished a project because they feared, expected, and ultimately ensured their failure.

6

How to Manage Your Time Better

The problem with time is not that there is never enough of it; the problem is we don't know how to use time effectively. Taught that the past is something we can make up for (we can't) and that tomorrow will bring a better day (it won't), we fail to place on time the value it deserves.

We've also been told that time is money but, if we truly measured our time that way, we'd realize that yesterday has about as much currency as a canceled check, tomorrow holds no more promise than an IOU, and that the only cash readily available to us is what we have in the bank right now.

To invest wisely in the present and to ensure greater returns in the future requires analysis, planning, and action.

Analysis. The best way to discover where your time goes is to take an objective look at how you spend it. For the next week, keep a log of all your activities. Divide each day (include the weekend) into one-hour time segments. As you complete each activity, record in your log what you did and how long it took you to complete each particular activity. Then note next to your most important activities your feelings about how you used your time. Was your time well-spent, or did you waste your time? Was your energy level high or low? What people robbed you of your time and what people made you feel as if the value of your time was increased?

At the end of the week, determine and record on a summary sheet the amount of time you spent on each of your various activities: how much time on the phone, how much writing letters, how much meeting with people, how much attending formal meetings, how much exercising, how much relaxing by yourself, how much participating in family activities, and so on. You decide the categories. Your summary sheet will tell you the amount of time you devoted to each type of activity.

Next, see if there are any patterns in your written responses. Is your energy level generally higher in the morning or in the late afternoon? If there's a pattern, consider working on your most important projects when your energy level is highest. Is most of your quality time spent with or away from people? Maybe you prefer to work alone. Or maybe you hate being alone and grab for the phone more often than you should. Are there any regular activities you can combine or any that you can break into smaller segments to handle more effectively? Both practices will save you time. What did you do that wasn't necessary? Can you avoid doing these things again? Was there anything that could have been done faster? More efficiently? How much time did you spend on important activities? How much on unimportant ones?

Separate the activities in which your time was well spent (the time savers) from those in which your time was not well spent (the time wasters).How can you change your behavior to make the most of your time?

Plan. Time management, like any other kind of management, works best when it's well planned. To create your plan, examine your log from the viewpoint of the necessary (what you must do to reach your goals) the important (what will help you but isn't critical to your success) and the optional (what isn't necessary but wouldn't hurt you either). Your conclusions will make up your list of priorities.

Now decide how you can devote more time to doing what's necessary and less time to doing what's optional. Save your optional activities for those periods when time has been created by the efficient completion of a necessary or important task.

Action. Acting quickly, decisively, and effectively on the priorities established in your plan will replace the stress caused by your never having enough time with the healthy tension of feeling enthused about the ways you've taken advantage of your time. To make your time work for you, you must eliminate the time wasters and implement the time savers.

Here's how:

Clear your desk. Get as much clutter off your desk and into the wastepaper basket or on to someone else's desk (read: delegate) as soon as you can. Create a "Rip and Read" file for those articles that you want to read by ripping the necessary articles out of those magazines that are piling up, place them in a file folder, and throw away the magazine. When you go to lunch or a dentist appointment or a meeting where you know you will have to wait, bring the folder with you. Read the articles then.

Limit the work area of your desktop to the project you're working on at any one time. Keep what tools and resources you need within easy reach and return them to their designated places when you are through with them.

At the end of the day, clear your desk of everything but the one project you want to work on the following morning. Maintain a separate project file for each major project.

Plan your day. To experience significant relief of stress due to too little time, divide your goals into long-term (more than one week) and short-term (less than one week). Be specific but not too elaborate with your long-term goals. Record all your due dates in your calendar. Enter your short-term goals on your weekly and daily to-do lists. Then divide your next day into segments of time with each segment devoted to a particular activity (include time for rewards, food, rest, and relaxation). Try to schedule your most important projects at those times of the day when your energy level is highest. Of course there will be interruptions, but you'll handle these interruptions faster and more effectively if you're adhering to a schedule.

Without a schedule, you're just floundering. You're placing yourself at the mercy of whatever happens to come up. Instead of focusing on opportunities, you're responding to problems, circumstances, and the needs of others. With a schedule, you're giving your projects direction, reducing the chances for a crisis, working toward your goals, and creating time to enjoy the rewards of your achievements.

Create a to-do list. Make a list of what you want to work on, prioritize your list by order of importance, coordinate the activities on your to-do list with the time segments allocated in your time schedule. The end of each time segment can serve as a minideadline for whatever task you want to work on. Check your list periodically during the day for the satisfaction of seeing what you've accomplished, measuring how well you are using your time, and determining any adjustments you may wish to make.

Add to your list whenever necessary. Your to-do list should never be stagnant. There should always be something to cross off when completed, always something to add. If not for that day, for the next. keeping your list updated helps you be flexible and prepared to change when new opportunities present themselves.

Work on what's important. Working on your most important tasks prevents projects from getting out of hand. When a project becomes a crisis, the opportunities for mistakes are greater. Work on what's important and aim to beat your deadlines.

By staying ahead in the game of time, your create time not only for the unexpected but also for the urgent but not terribly important meeting, telephone call, and whim of your boss.

Set deadlines. Deadlines for each task will help you get started sooner, produce more in a shorter period of time, limit delays caused by perfectionism and, because deadlines force you to focus, you'll produce better quality work. Enter on your calendar your final deadline as well as any minideadlines leading up to the date when your project is due. Your list of daily activities can also include deadlines. Call them microdeadlines?

Focus on one thing at a time. Working on one thing at a time helps you complete more tasks. Choose the project that's most important to you, create a step-by-step approach to completing the project, set deadlines for the completion of each of your steps, and stick with each task until it is done. The more tasks you complete, the more accomplished you'll feel and the happier you'll be at the end of the day.

Reward yourself. Don't undermine your effort by forgetting to reward yourself. Instead of using coffee breaks, shopping, trips to the deli, and chatting with others as opportunities to avoid work, consider using them as rewards for work done. You'll not only complete more projects, you'll enjoy your breaks more.

Don't work for too long. More than 50 minutes without a break often leads to diminishing returns. The most effective and best quality work is usually done in short spurts of energy with frequent breaks in between.

If you have to work overtime, consider coming to the office early (when there are fewer distractions) rather than staying late (when you can give the impression that you're not in control).

Learn to say "No." As difficult as this may be (and it can be done nicely), you have to learn to say "no." Otherwise, your time will be managed by the wants, needs, and demands of others. Here are some ways to say "no" without making your listener feel rejected:

- "I'm so glad you dropped in, but I can't delay what I'm working on now. Can we talk about it later today? Say about 3?"

- "I'm happy to do that for you, but can it wait until I finish what I'm working on? I don't think it will take more than another hour?"
- "I wish I could help you, but I won't have a minute of free time until late tomorrow. Would you like to get together then?"

While making any of these statements it often helps to continue working while you're talking.

Delegate. If you're in a position of authority, see if you have some tasks that can be done by others. When delegating a task, be sure to clarify the levels of responsibility and authority. Most people left to their own devices will do too little rather than too much.

If you're not in a position of authority, perhaps you can swap some of your tasks with a coworker. Maybe there are some things you don't like to do that your coworker enjoys; maybe you can complete a coworker's troublesome task in less time than he or she can. The time you save by sharing responsibilities with another frees you to devote more energy to your more important projects. Sharing assignments can also cut down on boredom and burnout.

Liven up your dead time. Commuting, waiting for appointments, and eating lunch are all times that can be put to better use. Unless, of course, you don't want to put these times to better use. If these are times for rest and reflection, rest and reflect. If, however, you find yourself itching to work on an important project and frustrated by having to lose time to an activity that is not of high priority, consider keeping a file folder of dead time tasks. Articles to be read, itineraries to be constructed, bills to be paid, and projects to be brainstormed are only a few of the activities that can be done during any dead time.

Keep your dead time file handy so you can drop things in it throughout the day. And be sure to take it with you when you leave your office. There's nothing like waiting for an appointment with your dead time folder sitting on your desk.

Cut down on interruptions. Not everyone has a door to shut, a secretary to stand guard, or a phone that we can have take messages anytime that's convenient for us. To cut down on interruptions:

Rearrange your furniture. Put your desk or wherever you do most of your work as far away from your office door or cubicle entrance as possible. Then position it so that it doesn't face the entrance to where you work, and look busy. Sometimes people won't interrupt you if you look like you are working on something important. Especially if they've been told beforehand that there's work you have to get done by a certain time.

Head them off at the pass. Don't tell anyone to come see you whenever they have a problem. If someone does visit you, stand up to greet them and stay standing. Don't ask them to sit down. And don't be afraid to say, "Well, I have some things I have to take care of; I better get back to work." If necessary, consider walking toward your office door while you make these comments.

See them back at the ranch– theirs! In other words, get to them before they can get to you. That way you control your time. You determine when you want to visit and when you want to leave.

Establish a quiet hour. Ask your coworkers not to interrupt you during your first hour at the office. Explain that you need that time to work on special projects and prepare your plan for the day. Better yet: Recommend that have your company institute a quiet hour for everyone. An hour where outside calls should be answered, but no one can interrupt anyone else for any reason other than an emergency.

Lower a flag. Many companies have been able to increase productivity by giving to their employees an American flag on a stand with a six-inch staff. The flag can be moved up and down the staff by strings. Whenever an employee needs to work on something so important he or she can't be interrupted, the employee lowers the flag halfway down the staff. Everybody knows the code, and everybody obeys it.

Attach a sticker. This is an effective method for people who work in cubicles. At the entrance to your work station, place a colored sticker to indicate when you're working on something important and can't be interrupted. A red sticker can signal "Stay away" to your coworkers; a green one, "Come in." This method works best, however, when everyone in an office has stickers and obeys the code.

Institute a new open door policy. With this policy, the door is only open at certain established times during the day. You get more work done, free up greater blocks of time to talk with others, and give your colleagues some time to solve their own problems before coming to dump them on you.

Get back to work. When you are interrupted, return to the task you were working on and complete it. Do not start work on a new task.

Control your correspondence. The best way to get a grip on your mail is read all of it at one time and then answer all of it at one time. As you read each letter, think *TIME*:

T: *Throw away* whatever isn't important. Discard all but those memos and letters that have to be answered.

I: *Underline the most Important* parts of each memo and letter that has to be answered. This way you won't have to reread the whole letter, just the important parts.

M: *Make notes.* If a reply comes to mind while reading any memo or letter, make a note of it in the margin. When answering each memo or letter, consider opening with the note you made in the margin. That will help you get started faster and make your point sooner.

E: What's the most *Effective* way to answer this memo or letter? A phone call is faster than a letter reply and may save you time. On the other hand, a written reply is a permanent record, can be referred to later, and can serve as a reminder as it sits on your reader's desk.

When answering memos and letters, start with any form letters you might have on file, or create some. They save time and, when well written and updated, can be more effective than a letter that hasn't stood the test of time. For those letters that you don't have a predrafted reply, start with the easiest responses first. That will help you get started faster and, like an athlete before a game, warm you up for the more difficult pieces of correspondence later on.

After you've answered each memo or letter, immediately decide if you need to keep a record of the correspondence. Don't ask "Could we possibly ever use this?" Ask "Is it probable that we will ever need this?" Then dump anything that doesn't fall under the heading of "probable."

Tame your telephone. It's easier to telephone someone than to write, but it's not faster if you can't get off the phone. If you make all your telephone calls at one time during the day, each call that remains on your list will be an inducement to get off the phone and on with your next call.

Use a Rolodex to find quickly the numbers you want to call. Consider stapling the business cards of your important contacts to the cards in your Rolodex file. Use the back of the card for any important things you need to remember about that person. The names of his or spouse and kids, for example.

You can further reduce the time you spend on the phone by making a list of what you need to talk about before you make each call. That way you won't forget anything important, you'll know when it's time to get off the phone, and you can add to your list anything said by the person on the other end of the line.

Keep your introductory ice-breakers to a minimum. If you're calling someone, you can keep your introductory remarks from getting out of hand by saying something such as "Let me tell you why I called." If someone is calling you, try "It's so good to hear from you, how can I help you?" or "I'm really glad you called, what can can I do for you?"

To end any telephone conversation, keep your responses short (but not curt) and practice exits such as:

- "I'll let you get back to work."
- "I'm going to have to let you go; I was supposed to be in a meeting in five minutes."

If a person you want to talk to puts you on call waiting, have some task handy to work on. Or, if you have things you need to do, ask if you can call back at a more convenient time. You can also give your listener the option of calling you when he or she is free, but that takes the next step of action out of your control. Better to establish some specific time for any return call.

Go high tech. Use call waiting, call forwarding, and voice mail to limit interruptions; use the same and a fax machine to circumvent having to talk on the phone. Car phones and cellular phones can save you time when you're out of the office.

If you spend too much time on the phone without realizing it, stand up when you make your calls. When you get tired of standing, you'll get tired of talking. While standing, see if there aren't some things you can do with your hands, some mindless tasks that won't distract you from your conversation.

Head off the crisis. Nobody can anticipate and preempt every crisis, but you can cut down on the number and extent of the crises by learning from the past. Are there any patterns to the crises that have already occurred? What can be done to prevent these recurring crises from continuing? When planning a project, ask what is most likely to go wrong. What will I do when that most likely thing happens? Can I do something now to prevent this crisis?

Move those meetings. There are two kinds of meetings: yours and theirs.

Yours. If you're running a meeting, begin and end on time. To wait for those who haven't showed up on time is not fair to those who have. And those who know you'll wait will not hurry to make your meeting on time. If, however, you let it be known that you will start every meeting when you say it will start and you always do what you say, your chances of getting everyone to the meeting on time will be increased.

It's also important to end on time. People have work to do, and they've already allocated to you the time you've asked for. Don't abuse it. Consider scheduling your meeting just before noon. People will want to be encouraged to stick to the meeting's agenda so they won't lose time from their lunch break.

Theirs. If you're attending a meeting called by someone else, show up prepared and on time. Take your dead time folder with you in case the meeting is delayed. While the meeting is in progress, avoid prolonging any discussions by not saying the first thing that comes into your mind. The first thing to come to your mind is often the first thing to enter the mind of others. Say the second thing.

Also: Be open to the viewpoints of others, don't talk while someone else is speaking, use your body language to show that you care about what is being said, don't interrupt anyone who is speaking, don't leave the room or head for the coffee table while someone is speaking, don't dwell on the insignificant, don't smoke unless everyone has agreed to allow smoking, don't be defensive or argue too strongly against another opinion, don't eat in the meeting room (unless it's a luncheon meeting), don't always sit in the same place or next to the same person, and take the initiative in getting to know anyone you haven't met.

Pounce on that paperwork. You can cut down on your paperwork by vowing to handle each piece of paper only once. You won't always succeed, but you will save time by deciding as soon as you read any memo or letter what action you want to take and then doing it. Adding a task to your to-do list, by the way, or throwing a memo in your dead time folder is an action.

Play the accordion. Get an accordion file with at least 31 compartments and number the individual compartments (1 through 31). Think of each compartment standing for a separate day of the month. Place any assignment not requiring immediate action into the compartment corresponding to the day you want to work on that particular task. Check your accordion file every day to plan and prioritize your assignments for the next day.

Bust the busy work. Some of what we do is meaningless. Busy work is often used to fill up the time we have to spend at work. Before adding an item to your to do list, ask what would happen if you didn't complete this particular task. If your answer is "nothing" or "probably nothing," throw the assignment into tomorrow's compartment in your accordion file. If the task keeps moving from one day's compartment to the next without ever making it onto your to-do list, eliminate the task. The time you saved can be devoted to more important work.

Work on what's important. Working on your most important tasks prevents projects from getting out of control. When a project becomes a crisis, the opportunities for mistakes are increased. Work, then, on what's important and aim to beat your deadlines. By staying ahead in the game of time, you handle problems before they can reach the crisis state, reserve time for the urgent but not important meeting, or phone call, or boss's whim, and create time to resolve the unexpected interruptions.

Keep a record. A folder containing a record of your achievements as well as any commending letters you receive can be helpful when you prepare for a performance review or plan to ask for a promotion or a raise.

Enough time on time. Remember, time wasted is opportunity lost. Ask first and always, "What's the best way for me to use my time right now?"

7

How to Take
Control of
Your Projects

The key to managing any project successfully is to break the project down into three phases to work on one at a time; then break each of the three phases into smaller tasks that you can complete one at a time. The three phases are: Plan, Act, Review.

Plan

This first stage in the project-management process is crucial. The better the job you do in this preparation stage, the faster and easier the following phases will be.

So don't rush into completing the project. Take the time you need to study similar projects (What can you repeat? What mistakes can you learn from?) and discuss your findings and ideas with your friends and colleagues (They might suggest alternative strategies from their own experiences). Then, when you feel you have enough information to begin working on the specific project: Create a cluster.

Clustering is probably the world's fastest and most effective thinking technique. A form of brainstorming, *clustering* enables you to quickly record your ideas on paper and then, when they are all recorded, see them all at once. Being able to see your ideas all at once provides you with an overview; it enables you to be more objective about which ideas are effective and which are not.

To cluster your thoughts on any project, write the name of the project in the middle of a blank piece of paper and circle it. My cluster on how to brainstorm projects, for example, started out like this:

The next step is the most important. Add to your cluster the project-related thoughts that have been bouncing around inside your head since you began your research. Important: Don't try to think of things to cluster. You've been reading and talking about this project for some time now; you have some idea about what the project should entail. Allow these thoughts to enter your mind, then record them on the page. Only don't write these thoughts out in complete sentences; just note a few words to help you remember the idea, circle the idea, and connect that circle to whichever circle led to it. My cluster for writing about this process as a brainstorming technique, for example, looked like this:

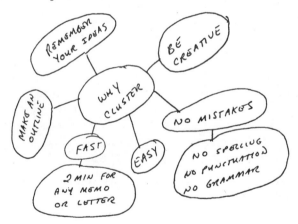

One of the great advantages of clustering is that it works the same way your mind does. It records your thoughts randomly, the way they enter your mind. Once your thoughts are on the page and you can see them all at once, you can put them into a list or outline. The thoughts could be listed in chronological order or in a step-by-step process or in any way that you think is most effective.

For the purposes of this chapter, the points in my list carry more or less equal weight:

Record all your thoughts. Whatever ideas come to mind, even if some of them are a little off or seem strange at the time, enter them into your cluster. Your mind knows where it's going even if you don't. If you take the risk of recording all your thoughts, even the the ones that are only indirectly related, you'll discover that your most creative solutions to problems and your most creative expressions of those solutions will come at those times when you go in the directions your mind wants to take you.

And it's not necessary to write out these thoughts in complete sentences. No one has to see or understand your cluster but you. Record just the number of words you need to remember the idea and then move on. Recording your ideas in a few words enables your hand to keep up with your mind. Not only, then, will clustering help you generate ideas; it also will help you remember them.

Don't judge your ideas. Don't discard ideas, just record them. Once they're on the page and you can see them all at once, you can eliminate the ones you don't need. Or combine them with others as I did with "Record all your thoughts" and "Don't judge your ideas."

It's okay to repeat an idea. This happens when we use different words that mean the same thing. Don't worry about it; what's important in clustering is to record all your project-related thoughts as they come into your mind. When you complete your cluster, you can eliminate any repetition.

Stop when the ideas stop. When you are finished with clustering, sit back in your chair, relax, and perhaps doodle with your cluster by running your pen or pencil over the circles in your cluster. Give your mind a chance to process a few more thoughts (minds need breaks too). If no further thoughts enter your consciousness, stop clustering and move on to the next step in the project-management process:

You can't make a mistake. No one has to see your cluster but you; no one has to understand what it means but you.

Act

To act effectively on any project requires the Right Attitude, namely, making whatever project you're working on your number one priority. To do what's necessary to complete your project well and on deadline requires constant time, attention, and motivation. In short, the project must become your obsession at work; all other priorities are put on the back burner until your project-related work for any given day is finished.

This Right Attitude will lead you to the Right Action (your cluster is your guide), and the number one Right Action for all projects regardless of their length or depth is *discipline, discipline, discipline.*

The word cannot be repeated enough.

Completing projects successfully and on time doesn't have all that much to do with intelligence (all project workers are intelligent; that's why they're assigned the projects) or knowledge (if you've done the research, you have the knowledge) or talent (a lot of very talented people never complete important projects). It has to do more with setting up a schedule of hours each day to devote to the project and sticking like glue to that schedule.

You know from your cluster and the step-by-step list you created from it what you have to do to complete your project. Estimate how long it will take you to finish each step, allocate the time you need each day to complete the project on deadline (give yourself an extra half hour at the end of each time period in case you get on a roll) and start working.

Monitor your performance every day by checking where you are in the step-by-step process and how far you have to go to complete a task. If corrective action is needed, take it. If you start to fall behind, create time in your overall work schedule to catch up, reevaluate the steps you brainstormed (perhaps some of them can be eliminated or combined with others) and, if you think you won't complete your project when it's due, inform your boss or supervisor as soon as possible (you don't want to blindside anyone with an unfinished product, and your boss or supervisor might suggest some alternatives).

Review

Reviewing your completed project gives you the opportunity to note the successes you want to repeat and the mistakes you want to avoid on future projects. Consider these questions when evaluating any completed project:

- What worked? What didn't? What can we we learn and implement in future projects?
- Was the project completed as planned? Were the original goals and objectives met? In what ways does the finished project differ from the way it was originally conceived?
- Was the completed project well received by supervisors and clients? Why? Why not?
- What measurements for monitoring progress on the project worked and didn't work? Why and why not?
- What backup solutions can be suggested for future projects of this kind?
- What could be done differently if the same project was assigned today?

8

How to Use Words That Work

Having a good vocabulary doesn't mean knowing a lot of big words. It means having the ability to express the same thought in different ways. So, if someone doesn't understand one way that we say something, we aren't stuck with having to repeat the words we used to communicate the message. We can use other words that mean the same thing.

Except for the jargon that is a part of our profession, a 10-year-old has most of the words needed to express what we want to say. The problem is not the number of words in our vocabularies but the ways we use these words. Many of the words we use work against our best interests. By developing the Right Attitude toward language, you can make your words work for you. Positive-sounding words (as opposed to negative-sounding words) help you not only say what you mean but also get what you want. Positive-sounding words such as "agree," "advantage," and "admirable" draw your readers and listeners closer to the message you want to convey. Negative-sounding words such as "overreaction," "questionable," and "disagree" make people want to distance themselves from you and possibly make them feel defensive.

The most important change you can make in developing a powerful vocabulary is to consciously change your negative- and neutral-sounding words into positive-sounding ones. Your writing is the easiest place to begin because, when you write, you have the opportunity to review and edit. But the habit you develop in your writing will soon carry over into your speaking, and what you say will quickly influence how you think and behave.

Start with the small words:

Can't

Instead of: I can't get you the report until . . .
Consider: I can get that report to you . . .
You'll have that report by . . .

Don't

Instead of: I don't agree . . .
Consider: I understand how you feel . . .
I can see why . . .
I agree with your point about . . .

Not

Instead of: That's not practical.
Consider: Let's give it a try.
What's the worst that could happen?

Have

Instead of: What you have to do is . . .
Consider: Here's one thing you can do to . . .
Have you thought of these alternatives?
What about trying . . . ?
Instead of: I have to . . .
Consider: I'm looking forward to . . .
I'm eager to . . .

But

Instead of: That was a good meeting, but . . .
Consider: That was a good meeting, and here are two things you can do
to conduct an even better meeting next month.

Must

Instead of: You must . . .
Consider: What do you think of . . . ?
Is there an alternative to . . . ?
Have you thought about trying . . . ?

Neutral sounding words can also be empowered:

Try

Instead of: I'll try to get this to you by . . .

Consider: I will get this to you by . . .

> You'll have it in your hands by . . .

May
Instead of: I'll try to be there by 2.
Consider: I'll be there before 3.

> Three gives me plenty of time.

Should
Instead of: I should be able give this to you by Wednesday.
Consider: I will give it to you before Friday.

> You'll have it by Friday noon.

Luck
Instead of: I got lucky on that one.
Consider: I worked hard on that project.

> Taking the risk on that call did it.

Hope
Instead of: I hope to be able to . . .
Consider: Count on seeing that by . . .

> You'll have it before . . .
>
> I'll take the responsibility of . . .

Like
Instead of: I'd like to . . .
Consider: I want to . . .

> I'd be happy to . . .

To strengthen phrases, think of what they mean and the impression you want them to have on your reader or listener. "To tell the truth," for example, gives the impression "I don't always tell the truth but this time I will." Just tell the truth and you won't have to announce when you're going to be honest. Same for "Let me be frank." Always be frank and sensitive to the needs and feelings of others.

Instead of: We have a problem.
Consider: Here's an opportunity to . . .

> If we can meet this challenge, . . .

Instead of: Can I bring anything?
Consider: What can I bring?

> What do you need me to bring?

Tell me how I can help.

Can I be responsible for . . . ?

Instead of: I'm no good at . . .

Consider: I'm getting better at . . .

I'm learning to . . .

I've discovered that . . .

Instead of: I wonder if you could . . .

Consider: When will you . . . ?

Here's something you can do to . . .

Please help me to . . .

Instead of: I spent my time . . .

Consider: I enjoyed . . .

I learned a lot from . . .

I benefited from . . .

Instead of: We tried that one before.

Consider: Let's give it another try.

What did we learn from the last time?.

What will make it work this time?

Instead of: Is everything okay?

Consider: What can we do to make this better?

How can I help you?

Instead of: I failed to . . .

Consider: Here's what I learned from . . .

The lesson on that project is . . .

I realized that . . .

I discovered it's not . . .

Instead of: One thing you might want to keep in mind is whether . . .

Consider: Think about whether . . .

Weigh your options.

Is it better to _____or _____?

Have you thought about . . . ?

You can't control all the circumstances in your life, but you can control to a great extent the image that others have of you. If you think positively and use positive-sounding words, your listeners and readers will think of you as a positive person. And people want to work with people whose outlook on life is positive. They know that positive people encourage cooperation and reduce conflict because of their willingness to consider fresh ideas and risk new solutions. And because they have confidence in themselves, positive people are also more likely to give credit to others.

Think, speak, write, and act positively. Others will judge you by your words and deeds and will prove you are the person you know yourself to be.

Part 2
Getting the Job You Want

Looking for a job is a job in itself. It takes creativity, resourcefulness, patience, discipline, courage, perseverance, and hard work. But all these qualities won't help you if you don't

Know what you want. Make a list of what you like to do, what you do well, and what experience you have from what you've done. Most people looking for a job begin with the want ads when they should begin with themselves.

Get organized. Approach your job search as if it were a project at work. Set goals and mini-goals, establish deadlines, keep that to do list active. You've got resumes to create (different jobs require different resumes), cover letters to write, resources to explore, and people to meet. You need to plan, prepare, and be ready to act. A regular schedule with specific blocks of time set aside for specific tasks will help you get organized and stay on track.

Hunt everyday. Treat your job search as if it really were a job. Unemployment is no vacation. Rise and shine the same as you would for any workday. If you don't have an office or space in your home where you can work uninterrupted, consider going to the library or using the spare office of a friend. The point is that you don't act when you happen to think of something to do. You actively hunt everyday for your job. Here's how:

Read the want ads. But avoid ads to which your response might be "That sounds like fun" or "This looks interesting." Look for what you like to do, what you do well, and what you've done in the past.

Think of your work experience in terms of the services or functions you've performed.

What machines did you operate? How much budgeting was required? Did you have to manage or train anyone? What communication skills were necessary? You might have been called an "administrative assistant," but you also might have been responsible for the day-to-day running of an entire office.

Talk to others. Let your friends and the contacts you've made through past work know that you're looking for a job; consider sending them a resume. You never know whom they might run into or what they might learn.

Contact the agencies. Most employment agencies charge the employer, so this probably won't cost you anything. Friends and business contacts might be able to recommend an agency they've worked with or put you in touch with a headhunter (someone who matches people with positions in specific professional fields).

Order more job lists. Most professional organizations periodically produce a list of jobs that are available in their particular fields. Or these organizations publish a magazine or newsletter that contains job listings. Many of these publications also include ads written by people looking for work but no study has been done on how successful these ads are.

Be flexible. There are more jobs to choose from if, for example, your willing to make some sacrifices or move to a different geographical area. No job, not even one 1000 miles away, will offer everything you want, but the more jobs you consider, the more opportunities you create to find a position that's closest to what you're looking for.

With a clear picture of what you want, a realistic appraisal of what you can do, a regular schedule to keep you active, and an open mind, you're ready to hunt.

9

How to Create an Eye-Catching Resume

No resume will land you a job; only you can do that. The purpose of your resume is to open doors, to grab a prospective employer's attention and make him or her want to interview you.

After your cover letter, your resume is your first big opportunity to make a good impression. Like you, it should be clean, neat, well-organized, error-free, and immediately accessible to anyone who wants to read it. You're in the wastepaper basket if your resume looks sloppy (i.e., has uneven margins, isn't centered on the page, lacks subject headings, looks as if it's been handled before, contains grammatical errors, is too short, too long [more than two pages unless you're in a profession that requires a *vita*], or contains irrelevant information).

Put yourself in the reader's place: You've got a job to fill and have to sift through the resumes of the people who've applied. All the resumes look the same and you're staring at 100 (not a high number) of them. The first step to eliminate the ones that don't look good and find out what's wrong with the rest.

Studies have shown that prospective employers give an average of 30 seconds (two minutes at the most) of serious consideration to any resume that aren't rejected on appearance or errors in the cover letter.

What do they look for?

Style. Does the resume look good on the page? Is the information clearly presented? Is it simple, straightforward, and easy to read?

Substance. Does the information on the resume match with the skills needed to do the job?

Here's how to combine *style* and *substance*:

Start with a name. Present it at the top of the first page in capital letters or boldface print. This shows that you're important, or at least more important than the applicants who list all but the initial letters of their names in lowercase.

Most professional resume consultants say to list your address and telephone number under your name; a few say this information takes away from the statement you want your boldly written name to make and can be included elsewhere in the resume. Still others say at least your name and possibly your address and phone number should head each resume page. You decide which format is most effective for you, but this is the standard:

MARK ROBBINS
709 Third Avenue
Brooklyn, New York, 11209
718-835-7535

Consider stating your career goal. If you think appearing ambitious will make you a more desirable candidate, you may wish to state your career goal. Employers often like people who want to get ahead.

On the other hand, they don't like to think of themselves as someone else's stepping stone. So you may wish to state a goal from among the positions that might eventually become available in the company you're writing to. Instead of stating "To run my own career placement agency," for example, you may wish to write "To run the human resources department of a large hospital."

Again, the choice is yours. Should you decide to list your career objective, be specific. "To work in sales" is not specific; "To direct a sales team for Berkeley Machines, Inc." is.

MARK ROBBINS
709 Third Avenue
Brooklyn, New York, 11209
718-836-7535

CAREER OBJECTIVE: To direct a sales team for Berkeley Machines, Inc., and write a book about successful career placement techniques.

List your work experience. Start with your most recent job and work toward your earliest. Include your job titles, the names of the companies you worked for, the dates you worked for these companies, and a brief description of your duties at each position you held. Emphasize how the work you did pertains to the job you're applying for.

When describing your duties, use "management verbs" to express your highest levels of achievement. Management verbs show that you're in charge or responsible for outcomes. You may have *worked* (not a management verb) as a sales clerk but, if you had to *organize* a sale you *performed* (both management verbs) functions on a higher level of achievement than your job title indicates. In other words, select verbs that show management experience and potential.

Here are a list of management verbs that will present the work you've done in its best light:

administered	generated
arranged	implemented
compiled	managed
coordinated	organized
created	planned
decided	prepared
designed	recommended
developed	solved
evaluated	trained

For example:

EXPERIENCE: Billing Manager. Interstate Trucking Company, Ames, Iowa (1989-present). Designed and implemented a computer billing system that reduced by 20 percent the time it took to issue a bill and saved Interstate more than $5000 in the first six months it was used.

If you think the work you did is of more interest to your prospective employer than the title of the position you held, consider stating your achievements first:

EXPERIENCE: Designed and implemented a computer billing system that reduced the time it took to issue a bill by 20 percent and saved the company more than $5000 in the first six months it was used. Billing Manager. Interstate Trucking Company, Ames, Iowa, 1989-present.

There are several effective formats to choose from when creating the look of your resume. Check them out at any photocopy center or printing business that has a resume-writing service.

List your formal education or training. Begin with your highest level of achievement. State your degrees first (they're more important than where you got them), the subject fields, the colleges or universities that you've graduated from and the years you graduated. If your work experience is limited, include any courses you took or internships you participated in that pertain to the job you're applying for.

List any awards or honors you may have received. Because the award is more important than the organization that bestowed it, list the award first. Any offices you may have held show leadership ability and peer respect. List the office before the organization. Your list of awards and offices can be included in the section with your degrees, or it can be presented in a category of its own.

EDUCATION: Master of Arts, English, New York University, 1992. Bachelor of Arts, English with a minor in Education. Loyola Marymount University, 1989. Magna Cum Laude.

President of the English Society, tutor in the university's Reach Out program.

If you hold a college degree, do not list your high school diploma. If your high school diploma is your highest level of academic achievement, list it the same way you would if you had graduated from a college. Be sure to state whether your diploma is academic, general, business, or manual arts.

EDUCATION: Odessa High School, Academic Diploma, 1985.

Provide references. It is not necessary to list them on your resume unless you need to fill up space (you don't want your references pestered by anyone who has an interest in hiring you). Instead, take the professional route and establish a dossier at the Career Placement Office in the school you last attended or, if they provide this service, at any professional organization of which you are a member. Ask each of the people writing a letter of recommendation for you (and they can write a better letter if they have a copy of your updated resume in hand) to mail his or her letter to the office holding your dossier. Once you've compiled a file of references, you can ask your prospective employers to write to the office where your dossier has been placed, or you can ask the office holding your dossier to send a copy of your references to your prospective employers.

Colleges and universities normally don't charge to maintain a dossier, and the fee charged by professional organizations rarely exceeds $50 for each year that your dossier is on file.

On your resume, then, you can list your references this way:

REFERENCES: A dossier of current and confidential letters of reference can be obtained by writing to:

Career Placement Office New York University Washington Square New York, NY 10011

Whom should you ask for a letter of recommendation? Someone who knows you and your work, thinks highly of you, carries some weight with your prospective employers, and who can articulate your accomplishments in a convincing way. A well-known name in your field is always impressive but not always as effective as a lesser-known authority who knows you better and will write more extensively about you.

Aim to have four first-rate letters of recommendation in your dossier.

Here're are some things not to put in your resume:

The date. All resumes are current.

Irrelevant information. Sports, hobbies, favorite foods, where you like to travel.

A photograph. If you're applying for a job in a foreign country where an in-person interview is unlikely, a photograph might help, but be careful how you submit it. To paperclip a photograph to a resume looks like you're applying for a driver's license. On the other hand, a photograph that has been professionally integrated with a resume (think of the business cards with photographs) might create too slick of an image in your readers' minds.

Your salary requirements. If you want too much, you may put yourself out of the running; too little and you're in a position to be taken advantage of. Find out the going rate for the position and wait until you're offered the job when you'll have more leverage to bargain.

Age, race, nationality, religion, sex, marital status, ancestry. There are laws against considering these characteristics as criteria for hiring, but that doesn't mean people in personnel aren't prejudiced toward the old, the infirm, women with children, and members of minority populations. On the other hand, many employers advocate affirmative action programs and look to hire women and people of color.

If you think you might have an advantage in landing a job because you're a member of a minority group, let your reader know subtly. For example, you might join the National Association for the Advancement of Colored People (NAACP), if you're not already a member and list it along with your membership in professional organizations.

MEMBERSHIPS: National Council of Teachers of English (regional vice-president), National Association for the Advancement of Colored People, Modern Language Association.

Here's an example of what a resume might look like:

MARK ROBBINS
709 Third Avenue
Brooklyn, New York, 11209
718-839 7535

CAREER OBJECTIVE: To earn a doctorate in education and become a curriculum specialist in a secondary school.

PROFESSIONAL
EXPERIENCE: English Teacher. Xaverian High School, Brooklyn, New York, 1989-present. Teach freshman composition and grammar, junior literature (an English survey course from *Beowulf* to Anita Brookner's *Hotel du Lac*). Also sit on the following committees: curriculum, faculty development, intramural sports. Each spring, I coach the men's cross-country track team. In 1990, I was voted Best New Teacher for my scores on the students' annual evaluations.

English Teacher. Public School 102, Brooklyn, New York, 1988-1989. Taught grammar and introduction to literature to sixth- and seventh-grade students.

Teacher's Assistant. Zora Neale Hurston Junior High School, Watts, California. Helped in the preparation and execution of classroom lessons, corrected essays, and tutored slower students in remedial reading and writing for Loyola Marymount University's student Reach Out program.

EDUCATION: Master of Arts, English, New York University, 1992. Thesis: *Climbing Out of the Sewer: A Search for Alternatives in the Works of Richard Wright.*

Bachelor of Arts, English with a minor in education, Loyola Marymount University, 1989. Magna Cum Laude. President of the English Society, tutor in the university's Reach Out program.

TRAINING:	New York City Secondary School Certification, 1990.
AWARDS:	New York State Regents Scholar, 1988-1992.
	The Ralph Ellison Award, New York University, for promising work in the field of African-American studies, 1988.
PUBLICATION:	"The Treatment of White Women in the Early Works of Alice Walker." *Southern Humanities Review*, Spring Issue, 1988.
REFERENCES:	A dossier of current and confidential letters of reference may be obtained by writing to:
	Career Placement Services New York University Washington Square New York, NY 100111
MEMBERSHIPS:	Modern Language Association, National Association for the Advancement of Colored People, National Council of Teachers of English.

Some Final Thoughts on Resumes

Play it safe. When it comes to resumes, as with so much else in life, the conservative approach is usually the most effective. To deviate too much in any one direction from the norm often makes interviewers wary. And if they're to be held accountable for the hiring decisions they make or the people they recommend, they'll be playing it safe too.

Update your achievements. Update every six months. And keep it in a folder with other records of your success: the new skills you've learned, job-related courses you've taken, workshops you've attended, and any letters of appreciation you've received.

Whenever you're due for a promotion, raise, or review, look over your updated resume and the notes in your file.

Bring copies of your resume to your interview. If, at the interview, you're asked to fill out an application form, your resume will help you complete it accurately. Extra copies of your resume can also be given to any interviewers who don't have one. This will refresh their memories and provide them with leads to follow when asking questions.

10

How to Write a Cover Letter That Gets Read

Your cover letter is your first opportunity to make a good impression. If your letter is poorly organized or fails to show how your skills pertain to the job you're applying for, you appear disorganized or unfocused. If your letter contains misspelled words or grammatical errors, you come across as stupid or careless. To create a resume that makes you look your best:

Find a name. Many job advertisements provide the name of the person to whom you should address your letter. If, however, only a title (Chair of the Search Committee) or office (Department of Human Resources) is given, telephone the company or institution you're writing to and ask for the name of the person in charge of the search committee or personnel department.

If you send your letter to a specific person and spell that person's name correctly, you have a reader who's on your side before he or she reads the first word.

And while you're on the phone, see if you can't have a brochure or annual report sent to you. You might learn something about the company's goals, policies, and achievements. Then, in your cover letter, show how you can contribute to the company's success.

If no information is available, ask to speak to someone in personnel. Identify yourself as a possible candidate for the available position and consider asking questions such as:

- What does this company do?
- What services does it provide?

- How large is it?
- How did it get started?
- Is it family owned?
- Are there branches in other cities?
- Is it growing or conserving?
- Are the employees generally happy?
- What benefits does the company offer?
- Are the salaries competitive?

These may seem like tough questions, but company employees (and not necessarily those weighing your candidacy) can provide many of the answers. Some questions, or answers, rather, may have to wait for an interview. The more you can learn about any organization, the more ways you have to influence the people in it.

Get to the point. Get to the point quickly.

When responding to a published advertisement:

- Please consider me for the comptroller position.
- I read with great interest your recent notice in *The Washington Post* and wish to be considered for the travel agent position.

When following a lead:

- During the recent ADA convention in Chicago, Dr. Marge Dilliard, a dentist in your clinic, told me of your possible need for a dental assistant.

When writing a letter of inquiry:

- I'm looking for a position in engineering that will enable me to use my extensive computer skills. Might there be such an opening in your company?

Although many jobs are landed through leads and letters of inquiry, most jobs come from notices. In this case, your reader is interested in you only insofar as you qualify for the job described in the advertisement. Your cover letter, then, should stress how your skills, education, and work experience match what the reader is looking for. Let the advertisement be your guide and look to tailor the highlights of your resume into the qualifications they seek.

Keep it short. Cover letters should be no longer than one page unless absolutely necessary. Your task in your cover letter is to show how well you match the requirements stated in the job advertisement and, as a result, make your reader want to take a serious look at your resume. In other words, you want to grab your reader's attention and make him or her want to read more. So stress what you think will interest the reader the most. Landing a job at this point isn't so important as whetting an appetite.

In addition to presenting your most relevant experience, consider mentioning at least one way you can contribute to the company's goals (as gleaned from the brochure you requested). And be sure to include any special qualifications not mentioned in your resume.

Ask for an interview. This can be done by saying when you are available, mentioning where and when you can be reached if your reader wishes to contact you, or proposing to telephone the reader (give a day and time) to learn his or her response to your cover letter and resume.

Because all resumes look so similar, you want to stand out as a person in your cover letter. Write in the same voice that you would use if you were speaking to your reader on the telephone. The voice you use on the phone when speaking to clients, customers, or colleagues should be just like you: natural and professional.

Here's an example of what your cover letter might look like:

19 September 19xx

Ms. Pam Jackson
Office of Human Resources
Macy's Department Store
Herald Square
New York, NY 10015

Dear Ms. Jackson:

Please consider me for the department manager position.

My nine years of sales experience includes everything from promoting department sales to creating successful marketing strategies. For the past three years, my work as an assistant manager in Lord and Taylor's Junior Miss department has given me the opportunity to learn the skills necessary to plan, organize, and administer a department of my own. I'm also the person always chosen to train and supervise any new employees for the fifth floor.

This experience, along with my Associate of Arts degree from the Fashion Institute of Technology and my continued interest since childhood in the fashion industry, have prepared me to meet the challenges of the job you described in today's *New York Times*.

I also know from my contacts in the field that Macy's looks for people who have the intelligence and ambition to move up in the company. The enclosed resume demonstrates just how far and how fast I've been able to develop since entering the work force, and I am eager to bring to Macy's that same high level of energy and know-how. When I finish my Bachelor of Arts degree in marketing from the City University of New York, I will be prepared to accept even greater challenges and responsibilities.

Ms. Jackson, I thank you for your time and consideration and will call you next Thursday morning to see if you would like to meet with me and talk further about the possibility of my coming to Macy's.
Sincerely,

Sharon Doyle
441 East 7th Street, Apt. 3A
New York, NY 10010

212-256-3435

Although this letter has five paragraphs, you can see that, like most letters of application, it is divided into three parts: (1) refer to the job, (2) state your qualifications, and (3) conclude with the mechanics of noting that your resume is enclosed and you'd like to make arrangements for an interview.

11

How to Make Every Interview a Success

The interview may be the most stressful part of any job search, but it also contains the most opportunities for success. For the first time, you're more than words on a page. You're the person who's going to confirm your interviewer's wise choice to meet with you.

The problem, of course, is the interviewer's other wise choices. At this point in the hiring process, all the prospective candidates are more or less equal. All have similar backgrounds, skills, and interests. On paper, any one them could do the job. The interviewer's task is to determine the best match. What you say and do will either make or break you.

That's pressure.

And because of the pressure, you'll probably be nervous. That's okay. Interviewers expect you to be a little nervous; you wouldn't be normal if you weren't. But they also expect, once the interview is underway, for your nervousness to subside and be replaced by an almost intangible melding of confidence, enthusiasm, humility, and self-respect.

So if you can't relax, try to look relaxed. If you can appear relaxed, you'll give the impression of being confident. To instill confidence in yourself and be able to project your confidence to others, you must prepare thoroughly for each of the three stages of any interview: before, during, and after.

Before Your Interview

How well you prepare for any interview will go a long way toward determining whether your candidacy will be a success. To give yourself the best possible chance of landing any job:

Conduct research. The more you know about the job and the organization you want to work for, the more ways you'll have of influencing your interviewers. Ask someone in personnel for a brochure, catalogue, or an annual report. Talk to a current or former employee. The more you find out, the more clues you'll have as to what they're looking for. You'll not only be better able to tailor the relevant parts of your experience to their specific needs and wants, you'll also be able to ask more intelligent and perceptive questions than the candidate who has to ask what your questions demonstrate you already know. To impress your interviewers with the quality of your research, consider these approaches:

- After stating something that shows you know how the company was founded, ask how its focus has shifted since then.

- After mentioning the last president's long tenure, ask if management since then has been fairly stable.

- After recalling what you read about the company in the press, ask what your interviewers think about how the story was handled.

- After complementing the company on a recent success, ask what the company plans next.

The important thing here is that these approaches not seem rehearsed. Look for openings in your conversations to demonstrate your knowledge and ability to ask perceptive questions.

Make a list of the points you want to raise, bring the list to your interview, and use the time while waiting for your contact to review them. Do not refer to them once the interview begins.

Practice with friends. Form a panel of friends to ask you the kinds of questions you might expect at your interview. Think of your responses from their viewpoints. The answer that sank Raymond Bork's nomination for the Supreme Court was, when asked why he wanted to be a Justice, he replied, "I like new challenges." The interviewing panel had hoped for something a little more noble.

Here are the kinds of questions you might expect at your interview:

- What can you tell us about yourself?

- Why do you want this job?
- Why do you want to leave your present job?

Try to put yourself in a positive light on this one; don't badmouth your employer or the company: "The position limited my abilities."

- What would you like to know about this company?
- What do you look for in the people you want to work with?
- Where do you want to be five years from now?
- What are your major strengths?
- What's your biggest weakness?

Lie. Choose any negative that you can turn to your advantage: "I take my career too seriously," for example, or "I put too much pressure on myself to achieve."

- What conflicts have you resolved?
- What challenges you the most?
- What frustrates you?

Don't say, "Questions that sound as if they came out of a book on how to interview people." Again, find a negative that you can turn into a positive.

- How have you gotten along with your past supervisors?
- What do you do in your spare time?

Beware of questions like this last one. They're loaded. You think you're talking about something not related to work and they're wondering if you're interesting to spend time with.

Dress right. Appearance alone won't land you any job, but it can quickly eliminate you from consideration. So play it safe. Dress up but dress conservatively: natural colors and fibers, real leather, expensive but not ostentatious jewelry, and a simple, natural hairstyle.

Be organized. Carry extra copies of your resume with you to the interview (for those who haven't seen or it or left their copy at their desks), copies of your list of references (complete with names, addresses, telephone numbers, and perhaps a personal statement about how you know each one), and a pad and pencil (you never know what you need to be prepared for).

Arrive early and alone. Give ample time for bad weather, traffic delays, and the unfamiliar address. Warmly greet any receptionist or secretary (their influence cannot be underestimated). Use the time before your interview to look over any notes you've made on your research and any questions you want to ask your interviewers.

During Your Interview

Most interviewers claim they can tell in the first five minutes when a candidate is not right for the job. Here's what you can do to get past those crucial first five minutes:

Look good. Not just in the clothes you wear but in how you carry yourself. Greet everyone warmly and genuinely, shake their hands firmly, remember their names (repeating aloud each name as you hear it will help you), and don't sit down until asked. Be enthusiastic but not desperate and leave all your negative feelings at home.

Act like a colleague. These people aren't doing you a favor by asking you be inteviewed. To enter any interview with a hat-in-your-hand attitude is to undermine yourself right from the beginning. Your interviewer will think you're desperate and willing to take any job. Nor should you think of your interview as an oral examintion. Your interview is a reciprochal exchange between colleagues in the same field. You want to find out if you want to work with your prospective employers as much as they want to find if they can work with you.

Listen. Don't be in too much of a hurry to talk. Concentrate on what you're being told by maintaining eye contact, leaning slightly toward whomever is speaking, and showing signs of affirmation (e.g., nodding your head, saying things such as "Yes" and "I like that," rephrasing in your own words the major points that are presented to you, and not interrupting anyone at any time).

Speak. Take advantage of any opportunities to communicate your strengths, but be sure to ask questions that show how much you know about the company. This will demonstrate how interested you are in them. When asked questions:

Be succinct. Always try to say more than just "yes" or "no." Think "competent" and "compatible" and you will be better able to keep your responses to the point without saying more than your interviewers want to hear.

Be specific. Not "I like to work with people" but "My running the billing department at Allstate gave me the opportunity to . . ."

Avoid the negative. Don't say anything bad about a former employer or company. If you have to say something negative, try to focus on the unfair situation or the volatile issue rather than on anyone's personality.

If asked to say something about yourself (your leaving a job after only six months, for example), try to present yourself in a favorable light: "The job didn't offer the challenges I had expected" or "I quickly discovered there was little room for advancement."

Use management verbs. Focusing on your accomplishments rather than your duties will help you use management verbs. Instead of "I was a bill collector," try "I settled 200 individual accounts my first six months on the job and, by the end of my first year, was heading a team that developed strategies for corporate delinquents."

Let your interviewers be your guide. They're the ones with the agenda, so follow their lead and wait for the openings to say what you want them to hear. Do this naturally. If you too consciously search for chances to tout your accomplishments, you'll come across as self-centered and not caring about what others have to say.

Ask questions. Successful candidates always ask questions. Questions show your degree of interest in the company, your knowledge of the field, and your ability to analyze the information you've been given. A healthy set of questions also shows your interviewers that you're not so desperate that you'll take any job you can get. You want to know, if you're hired, your specific responsibilities, some of the details of your first project, whom you will report to, how your performance will be evaluated, how the job has been done in the past, what your interviewers are looking for in the person they hire, how they think you can help the company grow, and what opportunities for advancement await you.

Avoid salary. This is not always easy to do, but you want to delay any discussion of salary (other than its range) until you're offered the job. You'll have more leverage then and can use your weight to ask further about health benefits, retirement plans, stock options, bonuses, profit-sharing schemes, relocation allowances, and more.

Before the interview, discover what the average salary is for someone holding a position similar to the one you're applying for. If you have to talk money, you'll know what your boundaries are likely to be.

Deflect the illegal. As much as we like to talk about ourselves, your interviewers (with few exceptions) are forbidden by law to ask you questions concerning:

- your marital status
- the number of children you have

- the number of people you support
- your age
- whether you are or plan to become pregnant
- whether you practice birth control
- your marital status or what your spouse does for a living
- your birthplace
- citizenship
- medical conditions
- your unemployment compensation or welfare history
- religious beliefs, or what religious holidays you observe
- criminal or bond record
- your credit situation
- club or organization membership

If asked a question about one of these subjects and you believe to answer it is not in your best interest, you can sidestep the question by:

Shifting the focus. If, for example, you're asked if your family will object to your being on the road, you can ask how much traveling the job requires.

Answering with a question. If, for example, you're asked if you can make satisfactory child-care arrangements, you can say that you don't allow your personal life to interfere with your work and then ask how your interviewer has solved this problem. Can he or she recommend a day-care center?

Challenging the interviewer. This should be done only as a last resort and so tactfully that your interviewer should only be able to question whether he or she has been confronted. If, for example, your interviewer asks if you plan to have children, you can respond, "Only if motherhood is a requirement for the job."

Create that chemistry. An almost herculean task, but that's what your interviewers are looking for: the special spark that tells them "This is a match!" Increase your chances of success in this area by concentrating not on landing the job (that only leads you in hit or miss directions) but on demonstrating how you and the job are a perfect fit, how your qualifications and energy match your interviewers' image of who they want in the advertised position. On no account try to be something you're not. If you get the job, you'll fail to live up to the expectations you created in your interview; if you don't get the job you'll always wonder if you would have received an offer had you just been yourself.

After the Interview

Most of what takes place next will be out of your control, but you can continue to influence any decision by writing a separate "thank you" note to each of your interviewers. This shows how thoughtful and considerate you are, especially if you can build on some personal connection you've made with each interviewer. Write your letters within 24 hours of your interview as you want to keep your name fresh in their minds.

If you think it appropriate, you might ask in your letter a question of each interviewer in the hope of getting a response. A response could indicate serious consideration or, if you don't get the job, a possible future contact in the field.

While waiting for the good news, record your reactions to your interview in a notebook: what went well that you can repeat in other interviews, what mistakes can you learn from, and what questions gave you the most trouble.

If you're not offered the job, telephone one of your interviewers to learn what you can do better in future interviews. Don't complain.

Part 3

Developing Your Personal Communication Skills

The human mind, once stretched to a new
idea, never goes back to its original dimension.
OLIVER WENDELL HOLMES

12

How to Improve Your Writing Skills

When we were taught to write, we were taught to do three things simultaneously: *think* what you want to say, *write* it down on a piece of paper, and get it *correct* the first time because, if you wrote it correctly the first time, there would be fewer changes to make when you proofread and edited what you'd written. But it's very difficult to think, write, and correct at the same time. Our minds aren't programmed to perform three separate brain functions simultaneously.

Now there's a new way of writing that will improve the quality of your writing and cut the time you now spend thinking, writing, and correcting in half. This new way of writing takes the traditional process of performing three functions simultaneously and breaks it down into three separate steps done one at a time. First you think; then you write; then you correct.

Here's how to do it:

Think

"Clustering," the world's most effective brainstorming technique (see pp. 32–33), is a also a creative writing exercise.

> *Step 1.* Write in the middle of a blank piece of paper the name of the person, place, product, service, or idea that you want to write about. Then draw a circle around the name of your subject. If, for example, I wanted to write an article about why people should cluster, my cluster would start out looking something like this:

Step 2. After you've written the name of your subject in the middle of the
page and circled it, sit back and relax. Whatever thoughts come into
your mind about the subject, add them to your cluster. Don't *try* to think
of something to say. If you're writing a memo, letter, report, or
proposal, you have some idea of what you want to say. Let those
thoughts come into your mind without any force or prompting. Then,
as they enter your mind, record them on the page. When you record
them, don't write out your thoughts in complete sentences. Just use
one or two words to help you remember the idea.

My thoughts for an article about clustering, then, might very well
look something like this:

Step 3. Once you have your thoughts onto the page, organize them into
an outline. And you can put your outline right on the very same page
that you created cluster. Think of each set of clusters as a separate
paragraph in whatever memo, letter, report, or proposal you want to
write.

Now that you have your thoughts on the page and ordered them into an outline, you're ready to:

Write

Just as you learned to think through a creative process known as "clustering," now you're going to learn to write through a creative process known as "free writing." When you free write, you free yourself from all those correcting influences that slow you down and make writing such a chore. When you free write, you don't worry about spelling, punctuation, or grammar. In fact, you don't worry about making a mistake of any kind; you just write what you want to say in the same words you would use if you were speaking to your reader. And you let your outlined cluster be your guide.

Here's how:

Step 1. Put your pen on the page or your fingers on your keyboard. Start writing whatever you want to say about the idea that you've circled in the cluster marked as the first paragraph in your memo, letter, report, or proposal. For example, the cluster that I marked as #1 was "creative." My free writing of that thought might look something like this:

Clustering helps me be creative because it takes away all that pressure of having to be correct. Because my mind doesn't have to worry about spelling, punctuation, and grammar, it's free to think about what I want to say and how I want to say it. Once my words are on the page, then I can go back, edit them to improve my writing style, and make sure what I say is mechanically correct.

Step 2. After you write everything that comes to mind about what's in the cluster you've labeled #1, you relax for a few seconds, take the idea in the cluster you've labeled #2, begin a new paragraph, and write whatever you want to say about what's listed in cluster #2. Then you repeat this process with each cluster representing for a separate paragraph.

Once you've placed your thoughts on the page, organized them into an outline, and written them in a voice that is as close as possible to the way you speak, you're ready to:

Correct

Proofread everything you've written three times: for meaning, power, and correctness.

Proofread for meaning. To proofread for meaning, you read whatever you've written the same way your reader would: from beginning to end without stopping. The main thing you want to be concerned about is that your reader gets the message. Is it clear? Is it simple, straightforward, and easy to understand?

Proofread for power. After you're certain that your message is clear to your reader, look at:

Your opening sentence. Because your opening sentence determines whether your readers want to continue reading, it's the single most important sentence in anything you write.

How do you write a good opening sentence? You write it last. Once you've finished your freewriting, your words are on the page, you know what you've said, and you're close in time to what you've written, then you go back to the beginning and write your opening sentence.

Note: If you've free written as close as possible to the way that you speak, your original, free written, opening sentence will be satisfactory more than 90 percent of the time. Naturally, without any concentrated effort on your part, it will be short, simple, and easy to understand. The other 10 percent of the time you might want to change a word, add a punctuation mark, or perhaps rewrite the entire opening sentence.

If you decide to rewrite the entire opening sentence, consider using one of these four kinds of openings:

- The opening that gets right to the point.
- The opening that asks a question.
- The opening that presents a gripping fact.
- The opening that announces good news.

Proofread for correctness. To proofread for correctness, take a blank piece of paper and place it over all the lines of your memo or letter except the last line. Then read the last line backward from the right-hand margin to the left. When you reach the left-hand margin, move the bottom of the paper up to the next line. Then read that line backwards from right to left.

Moving backwards from the bottom to the top and from right to left takes the words out of the context in which you placed them and prevents you from getting caught up in the flow of the writing.

When you get to the top line of your memo or letter, you reverse the process. Cover all the lines of the memo or letter except the first line. Then read what you've written the normal way, from left to right. When you reach the right-hand margin, move the paper down to the next line. Don't move the paper until you reach the right-hand margin. This isn't speedreading; it's correct reading.

As you go down your memo or letter, you will discover all your misused words: the time you thought you wrote "their" and it came out "there," or the time you thought you wrote "form" and it came out "from."

Follow this three-step method (Think, Write, and Correct) and everything you write will contain all the basic principles of good writing.

You'll also cut your writing time in half. However much time you spend writing now will be cut in half by this three-step process and, if you're the kind of person who writes a lot (say, two or three hours a day), it's possible to cut your writing time down to a third of what it is now. Guaranteed!

13

How to Write Better Memos and Letters

Every memo and letter is an opportunity to make a good impression on someone and to present yourself as someone who can communicate in simple, clear, easy-to-understand prose.

Before writing any memo or letter:

Know your reader. The better you know your reader, the more ways you have of influencing him or her. Ask yourself: How does my reader think? How does my reader feel? What motivates my reader? What are my reader's biases and prejudices? If you only know the name of your reader and no one in your office can fill you in on him or her, put yourself in your reader's place. Ask yourself: From my reader's position in the company, how would I respond if I received a letter such as the one I'm sending?

Know what you're talking about. There's a big difference between having something to say and having to say something. Writers who know their subjects usually have something to say about them. When you know your subject well enough to explain it to someone not in your field, that's when you're to write about it. Use specific details about your subject to light a FIRE in your reader's imagination:

F. Facts.

I. Instances.

R. Reasons.

E. Examples.

It's the specific details that grab the strongest hold on our reader's imagination and last the longest. When we see a newspaper headline that informs us of an earthquake taking place somewhere in the world, we think "That's too bad," but when the next day's lead story tells us of a girl who's trapped at the bottom of a well and can be seen but not reached by her mother, the attention of the whole world is focused suddenly on the fate of that one child.

Memos and letters differ in format but they share the same style: simple, straightforward, easy to understand. To create the most effective style in any memo or letter, follow the three-step writing process discussed in the previous chapter. Then, once your words are on the page, consider editing what you've written into this three-part format:

1. *Why you're writing.* The purpose of any memo or letter should be stated early. If not in the first sentence, then in a second sentence that the opening sentence has made the reader want to read.

2. *What you want to say.* You want to say what your reader wants and needs to hear. To help you determine this, ask:

   - What does my reader know about this subject?
   - What more does my reader need to know?
   - What questions will my reader ask about what I am saying?

   Putting yourself in the reader's place and seeing what you've written from his or her point of view will help you determine not only what should go in any memo or letter but also the most effective tone of voice in which to state your message.

3. *What you want the reader to do.* Very often a writer will inform a reader about a particular subject but not say what he or she wants the reader to do. Tell your readers and be specific in your instructions. "As soon as possible" and "at your earliest convenience" are not specific. Specific is: "Larry, I need those figures on my desk by Tuesday morning at 10 a.m. because I'm going into a meeting at 11, and I have to go over those numbers before I go into that meeting. Please have them on my desk Tuesday morning at 10."

Although memos, because they're written to people in the same company we work for, can be more informal in style than letters, the major difference between them and letters is their format.

A Format for Memos

Most memos follow the same format, though they may be either printed or handwritten.

TO: All staff
FROM: Maria Lopez
SUBJECT: The broken photocopy machine
DATE: 21 May 19xx

    The message that follows in the space where you are now reading is usually written or printed flush left, but, because of their more informal nature, the beginning of each paragraph may also be indented. The important thing here is to be consistent. You wouldn't want to indent the opening of one paragraph and begin the next one flush left.

The most effective memos say first what's most important, state specifically what they want their readers to do, are written in clear sentences that don't have to be read twice to be understood, are kept short and to the point, and are free of errors.

Rarely is a memo more than one-page long.

A Format for Letters

The best business letters look good right from the very first second their readers glance at them. The paper is of good quality, there are no smudges or typographical errors, and the reader's name is always spelled correctly.

ON THE JOB, INC.
1040 North Pleasant Street
Amherst, Massachusetts, 01002

4 August 19xx

Ms. Gerardine Landry
United Bank
134 Old Conway Road
South Deerfield, MA 01059

    Dear Ms. Landry:

Not every letter has to look exactly alike, but every letter you write should follow the same format. So be consistent. If you write the date of one letter as "4 August 19xx," write the date of every letter this way. If you choose to indent the first line of every paragraph, indent the first line of every paragraph in every letter you write. This doesn't mean that you shouldn't experiment with different formats; it means that you should consistently use whatever format you choose until you discover a more effective one.

The best business letters are direct and to the point. They don't waste their readers' time by taking more than one page. But they are also written by human beings and are never curt or rude. Nor do they ever sound artificial. "Pursuant to our conversation" is not an expression you will ever find in a well-written business letter. Instead you will read, "Thank you for your telephone call today. Here's the information you asked for." Or "I enjoyed talking with you on the telephone today and am enclosing the report I promised you."

The best business letters make their point in the opening paragraph. The following paragraphs, regardless of the subject, are written in plain, simple, natural-sounding prose. The sentences are never stiff or dull. In fact, they remind the reader of the same voice they heard on the phone. Think of the people you like to hear from on the phone. Do they speak in clichés such as "As per" or "In reference to our previous conversation of"? The same is true for your readers. They want to hear from the same friendly, sincere, positive person they spoke to on the phone.

And that friendly, sincere, positive tone is carried all the way to the concluding paragraph. The best letters don't end with formalities such as "If you have any questions, please contact me" because the best writers know that too many letters end with "If you have any questions, please contact me." The best writers of the best letters show their readers that their telephone calls are important. The best writers tell their readers: "If you have any questions, please call me at 549-5328, the best time to reach me is before 10 a.m. on Monday, Wednesday, and Thursday." Or, if they don't think they're being too pushy, the best writers might end their letters with "I'll call you next Thursday morning to see what you think of my suggestion." These writers don't leave the next step of action up to the responsibility of the reader; they take it. They know that in an age of increasing dehumanization people are looking for human contacts, and provide their readers with those contacts. They establish and maintain human relationships with as many clients, customers, and colleagues as they can.

Sincerely,

Richard Andersen
President

P.S. Studies have shown that a hand-written postscript will be read twice by most readers— before and after they've read the body of the letter— but beware: a handwritten postscript can also create the impression that you're sloppy, forgetful, or disorganized.

Before Writing Any Memo or Letter Ask Yourself

Is what I've written personal? Have I used pronouns such as "you" and "I" instead of "one." If the tone of the letter doesn't require a certain level of formality, can I substitute contractions such as "I'm" for "I am" or "can't" for "cannot." Because we so often use them when we speak, contractions are a subtle way to draw your reader closer to your message and, at the same time, make you sound more personal and warm.

Have I called the person I'm writing to by name? Avoid, if possible, a "Dear Sir or Madam" salutation. Letters sent to specific people are answered faster and more effectively than letters sent to whomever opens the mail. Telephone the company you're writing to, get the name of a specific person, and spell that person's name correctly.

Are my ideas arranged effectively? Some letters require a chronological order, others a step-by-step process. If you can decide the order of your ideas, consider placing your most important idea first and your second most important idea last. People tend to remember best what they read first and second best what they read last.

Would any graphics help clarify my meaning. Visuals often aid your readers' understanding of a message. The best source for effective graphics is probably *USA Today*, but you can use headings, lists, tables, boldface, or underlines to emphasize and clarify what you want to say.

Have I eliminated all my clichés? Closely check the beginning and end of your letter. Instead of beginning "I acknowledge receipt of your letter of 19 September and wish to . . ." write, "Thank you for your letter of September 19th." In short, pretend the person you're writing to is sitting right in front of you at your desk. Whatever you would say to that person sitting right in front of you, say it the same way in your memo or letter.

Have I analyzed what I've written from the reader's point of view? Ask yourself: What's in this for my reader? Why should my reader agree with me? If I was reading this letter, would I want to be addressed in this tone of voice?

Have I used positive-sounding words? Instead of "We close at . . ." consider "We're here to serve you until . . ." Negative-sounding words such as "questionable" and "misinformed" make your readers want to distance themselves from you and your messages; words such as "agreeable" and "advantage" bring your readers closer.

Have I used natural-sounding words? Better to write "I'm the one you spoke to" (ending a sentence with a preposition), "And that's that" (beginning a sentence with a conjunction), "You're going to really enjoy Steve's presentation" (splitting an infinitive), and "Of the people, by the people, and for the people" (repeating a word) than search around for more correct but less effective constructions: "I'm the one to whom you spoke," "That is that," "You're going to enjoy really Steve's presentation," and "Of the people, by the persons, and for all the men, women, and children."

Have I kept the message short? Busy people don't have time to read long-winded letters. Keep your letters to no longer than one page unless absolutely necessary.

Am I consistent? If you've indented the first line of the first paragraph, indent the first line of each of the following paragraphs. If you've spelled the word "grey" with an "e," always spell it with an "e" in the same memo or letter. If you've used a comma before the "and" in "The flag was red, white, and blue," always use a comma before the "and" whenever you repeat that construction.

Am I correct? Double-check your nouns. Because nouns (the names of persons, places, and things) are where the information is, readers pay more attention to them than most of the other words. Make especially sure that all your nouns are spelled and used correctly.

Have I signed my name so people can read it? Your signature is the most personal part of your letter: Make it legible.

A Final Word About Writing

One model of an effective writing voice is the one you use when you speak on the telephone at work. When you speak to colleagues, clients, and customers on the phone, you don't use slang or idiomatic expressions that you use with other people at other times in your life. You also know from you experience on the phone at work what words are effective and what words aren't. You know what words will bring about one kind of reaction and what words will bring about another. So use in your writing the words you've already tested and proved. These words are not only natural, they're also professional.

14

How to Read Faster and Remember More

To Read Faster

Trust me: count the total number of lines on this page. Record that number here:_____.

When you counted the lines, did you use your finger or a pen or pencil? Most likely you did. Why? Because without your finger or an instrument to guide your eyes you know from experience that you increase your risk of missing a line or counting the same line twice.

And what is true for counting lines is also true for reading them. To read faster and more accurately, your eyes need a finger or some other kind of instrument to guide them. Speedreading specialists call this guide your "pacer."

Of all the kinds of pacers you have to choose from, a pencil is probably the most useful because it can be lowered to underline important passages and, if necessary, its marks can be erased.

Use your pacer to follow each line you read from left to right. When just beginning to develop your speedreading skills, keep your pacer moving at a rate that is slightly faster than the speed at which you are accustomed to reading. This will force you to read faster and, because you have to concentrate more to keep up with the pacer, you won't skip a line, read the same line twice, or be distracted by events or objects that appear out of the corners of your eyes. And because of your increased concentration, you will also remember better what you read. The participating act of underlining the most important passages will increase your retention ability even more.

When you reach the right-hand margin of any page you're reading, don't stop. Move your pacer quickly down to the next line. The faster and more smoothly you can move your pacer to the next line, the faster you will read. This method works best when you can feel a rhythm in the paces you set. Your eyes move quickly but never so quickly as to lessen your retention or so slow as to allow your mind to drift from the subject matter. Gracefully coordinating your hand, eyes, and mind in one smooth, fluid motion, you experience an effect not much different from driving your car at a high speed. In the same way that you allow the road's turns and grades to determine how much pressure you put on the gas pedal, so too do you decrease your speed when greater comprehension is required and increase it when the subject matter is less important. And like the expert driver who looks beyond his car's hood to those distant points in the road that provide the overview needed to anticipate changes, so too do you aim beyond any immediate word to the larger picture the words create in your mind.

One way of doing this is to focus on the nouns (what the information is) and the verbs (what the action is) and skim most of the other words. Compare, for example, the mental pictures created in your mind by the words "the," "an," and "a" with those created by any noun-verb combination that you can think of.

Speedreading is much like driving fast in another way: After a while, it becomes normal. Remember the feeling of cruising at 70 miles per hour and then having to slow down to 55? Fifty-five is not a slow speed, but it seems slow compared with the 70 we became accustomed to. The same is true of increasing and maintaining the speed at which you read. When you return to your average speed (around 250 words per minute for most people) you feel as if you're creeping along.

This is one of the reasons why professional speakers deliver their messages faster than people holding normal conversations. Speakers know that while most people converse at about 180 words a minute, they can absorb messages at up to 600 words a minute. So speakers often present their thoughts quickly and succinctly (250 words a minute is not uncommon) so their listeners' minds won't drift.

The same is true for good readers. By quickly absorbing the main ideas of any text, they learn more in a shorter period of time and, because they need to concentrate to keep pace with their reading rate, they remember more and retain it longer. Here are some additional tips for reading faster and remembering more:

Push yourself. Once you become comfortable reading at a certain speed, start moving your pacer slightly faster. Your eyes will adjust to the new speed just as they did to the previous increase. Never, however, read so fast as to make your eyes feel uncomfortable in their attempts to keep up with your pacer. Reading this fast lessens retention.

Don't consult your dictionary. At least not while you're reading. Try to guess the meaning of any word you don't understand from its context in the sentence. If you can create a mental picture of what you're reading early on and then fill in the details of that picture as you read, you'll increase your chances of correctly guessing the meaning of most unfamiliar words.

If you can't determine the meaning of any important word, circle it, dog-ear the page, and keep moving. When you finish reading, return to the word and look up its meaning in your dictionary.

Use your other hand. Keep a finger inserted in the next page of your text. As soon as you reach the bottom of any page, turn as quickly as you can to the next page. Many readers spend as much as 10 percent of their reading time just turning pages.

Don't read with your lips. If your lips move with the words you read or you find yourself mentally sounding any words, increase the pace of your reading speed until you don't have time to vocalize the words. If necessary, chew some candy or bite on a pen or pencil.

Be comfortable. Don't get too comfortable; a desk, unlike a bed or soft chair, keeps you looking down on your reading material. The resulting overview reduces any opportunities for your eyes to wander or grow tired and close.

Maintain the Right Attitude. Don't think of any reading material as "required" or "boring" or something that "has" to be read. If you do, you'll only notice what's boring in the text.

Avoid distractions. There are two kinds of distractions: external and internal.

External. Noise, deficient lighting, a cluttered desk, an uncomfortable chair, and more block concentration. Unless you need music to calm you down or drown out other noise, turn off your CD, radio, or tape player. You can't read faster and remember more when you're humming a tune or tapping your feet.

Internal. Internal distractions are the most difficult because you can't turn them off or move away from them. Studying for a final exam while worrying if you'll pass is a blueprint for failure. Know that if you follow the procedures detailed in this chapter, you will do better on any exam than if you used traditional study techniques and had all the time in the world.

Time yourself. Note how many pages you can read in a 10- or 15-minute span; and then see if you can beat your record. Once you become comfortable at the new pace, you have a new record to beat.

Establish deadlines. Tell yourself that you're going to read so many pages in such an amount of time. The pages (your goal) and the time (your deadline) will pressure you to read faster and concentrate more.

Practice. Speedreading is a skill. The more you do it, the better you get at it. By practicing frequently the mechanics of speedreading, you will quickly turn them into a habit and a part of your natural behavior.

Relax. Don't force yourself to read faster than you can comprehend the meaning of any words. Everybody is different, everybody reads at their own pace, and everybody can improve. Your goal is not to be the best speedreader that ever was but to better your skills to the highest level you can achieve.

Concentrate. "Concentrate" and "relax" are not contradictory. Unless you can relax (think of trying to read while you know deadlines await you in other areas, for example), you can't concentrate. Reading what interests you or finding something of interest in what you read increases your ability to concentrate.

Read for the main idea. Lengthy works of a not too technical nature can often be read effectively by reading the first lines of each paragraph. Another technique for longer works is to grasp the main idea and skip or skim the explications and case histories.

Expand your horizons. Don't limit yourself to a few subjects or writing styles. The more diverse your reading material, the more you know and the more capable you are at absorbing different kinds of information.

To Remember More

The traditional way to remember what we read is to underline the important parts of any text, then when we're ready to review the material.
Here's a better way:

Read the table of contents. The easier information enters your mind, the easier it is to retrieve. The table of contents of any book highlights what's important, gives your reading a direction or purpose, and provides you with a logical order to process information.

After you've read the table of contents, search for any summary, study questions, or illustrations pertaining to the chapter you're about to read. This material will further clarify the information you gleaned from the table of contents and help you focus better on what you need to know.

Read to fill in the details. You know the purpose of your reading from the table of contents and any study aids that might be included in the chapter. So look for the details in the text that reinforce that purpose. Concentrate on what you need to know to understand better the chapter's important points.

If a chapter is long or the material within it is complicated, don't read the entire chapter in one sitting. Read what you can and take a break. Because people tend to remember best what they read first afollowed by what they read last, you'll remember more by dividing your chapter into manageable sections of a few important points each. Reading by subject headings instead of by whole chapters increases your chances of remembering more material because a series of beginnings and endings related to one purpose provide you with more opportunities to learn than any text with one beginning and one ending and a large body of easy-to-be-forgotten material in the middle.

Dividing each chapter into manageable sections also helps you get started sooner (because short segments are less daunting than large chapters), read faster (your goal is always in sight), and improve your overall performance (because you are able to remember more from short, concentrated spurts of energy than longer, tiring segments of material that never seem to end).

Create a cluster. In the chapter entitled "How to Write," you learned clustering as a brainstorming technique, but clustering can also be used a memory device. When you come to the end of a chapter in any text you're reading, write the name of the subject or title of the chapter in the middle of a piece of paper. Then circle what you've written and begin clustering. A cluster of this chapter's section on speedreading, for example, might look something like this:

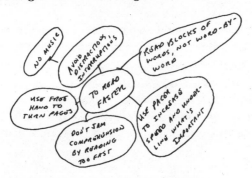

Because clustering forces you to recall and record what you think are the most important parts of any reading segment, you'll remember what any cluster means long after you created it. Keep your clusters inserted in the text at the end of whatever sections they pertain to. When it's time to review the material, open your text to the pages where the clusters are and study from the clusters.

Review your cluster. To move your recordings from your short-term memory bank to your long-term container, review your cluster within 10 minutes of having created it. Look at it again 24 hours later, a week later, and six months later. If you forget the meaning of any cluster, return to the pertaining section in the chapter and read what you've underlined. If you have to do this more than once, the forgotten material probably isn't as important as you once thought.

Not everything has to be read with the same level of concentration as a textbook, however. Here are some tips on how to handle other kinds of writing:

Magazines. Read the table of contents to decide what you want to read; then read each article in order of importance, starting with the most important first. If you want to keep an article and think a cluster is necessary, create your cluster on the article's title page or on the last page, wherever there's the most white space. Tear the article from the magazine and file it in an appropriate folder. Don't leave it sitting on your desk to serve as a distraction from whatever you're working on.

Newspapers. Go page by page rather than article by article. In other words, don't go from the lead page to the page where the story is continued then back to the lead page to begin another story. Read page by page, absorbing the information as you come across it. You'll remember where you left off in any story shortly after you've begun reading the continuation.

Letters. Before reading, divide your letters into two piles: those you know to be important and those you think may be important. Skim each important letter for its main idea and to determine whether the letter requires a deeper reading. Most letters won't. Then do the same for the letters that may be important. In both cases, look for what the writer wants, determine it's value to you, and quickly decide on what action you want to take.

Two Important Things to Remember About Remembering

1. There's no limit to what you can remember. Every word you've ever heard or read, every experience you've had or event you've participated

in is stored in the memory chamber of your mind. To recall these memories, all your mind needs is a trigger.

The trigger that is the basis of every memory recall system is called *association*. If you want to remember something new, the best way is to associate it with something old. What you choose to associate with any new idea can be either visual or verbal, but the strongest and most lasting associations are either emotionally charged or exaggerated to the point of absurdity. If you want to remember, for example, that a friend's birthday is on November 22, knowing that John Fitzgerald Kennedy died on November 22 will help you remember by association. If you want to remember that a new acquaintance is from New York, you can associate your friend with a Big Apple. If you want to remember a person's name, you can exaggerate one of the person's physical characteristics by turning it into an almost cartoon-like image and then rely on that image to trigger your memory, or you can rhyme a person's name with a similar-sounding word. If your rhyming word also contains a characterization of the person, you further increase your chances of remembering the name: "Mary-contrary," for example, or "Dave-brave."

2. You don't have to know everything. Read only those parts of a letter, report, or book that you need to read. Just to know a little is usually to know a lot more than anyone else. William James tells us, "The essence of genius is knowing what to overlook."

15

How to Listen to What You Hear

Hearing is a behavior; it's a physical act. Listening is a skill; it's a mental and emotional technique that enables us understand and, yes, even communicate without saying a word.

We hear more often than we do anything else except breathe. Yet, most of us listen at less than 25 percent of our potential. And much of what we want to pay attention to is forgotten, distorted, and misunderstood.

To listen effectively, you need to hear and select what's important, interpret its meaning, determine what you think about it, and reply.

To Hear and Select

Stop thinking of yourself. You are the single greatest barrier to being an effective listener. Caught up in thoughts of your own, you miss much of what is being communicated — and not just the words. They make up only 7 percent of most verbal messages. Voice inflection counts for 38 percent and the remaining 55 percent is totally nonverbal.

Choose to pay attention. Effective listening is not passive; it's active. Choose to listen actively and you quickly find yourself understanding better, appreciating your speakers more, and responding more effectively.

Assume responsibility. Increase your chances of a successful conversation by taking charge of it. Be prepared for any appointed meeting, show up on time, and be "present" once you get there. How many times have you been talking with a person and his or her mind is somewhere else. Try not to fidget, tap your feet, or look at your watch. If the choice of a meeting place is yours, choose a location without distractions (e.g., the telephone) or noise (e.g., a restaurant). If you're meeting in your office, come out from behind your desk (an authority barrier to communication) and stand or sit next to the person you're talking with. This sends the message that you really want to listen to what your speaker has to say.

Have the Right Attitude. If you enter a conversation with the attitude that the person is a bore, you will look for opportunities to confirm that viewpoint. You will only hear what's boring.

Having high expectations gives the other person a chance to be successful, and you can help any speaker improve his or her speaking ability simply by showing a genuine interest and asking sincere questions.

Visualize success. Practice for successful conversations by rehearsing how you will respond in specific situations: "If May says ... , then I'll say ...." Imagine yourself as a model of good listening. That's what you want to look like when someone is speaking to you.

Communicate while you're listening. Maintain eye contact, nod your head, show verbal approval, lean slightly forward, and put aside anything else you might be doing. These behaviors show you care about what your speaker has to say, and you help instill the confidence that many speakers need to explain their subjects in full.

Don't interrupt. When you interrupt someone who's speaking, you're sending the message that what you have to say is more important. Be patient. Even if your speaker is a windbag or someone who repeats the same thing several times, you have more to gain by waiting than you do from the few seconds you will save by interrupting.

Don't give in to boredom. Take responsibility for the direction of the conversation by determining how you can use the information the speaker presents. Ask questions that help the speaker address the issues of interest to you.

Listen for the hidden message. Very often, a psychological drama can take place during a conversation that has little to do with the words that are being spoken. A writer and an editor, for example, may be talking about ways to improve a letter, but the real issue may be power and who's going to have his or her own way.

Tone of voice (e.g., aggressive, pleading, reluctant) and body language (e.g., slouching, folded arms and legs, averted eyes) can convey as much as 70 percent of any speaker's message. Use your tone of voice (e.g., interested, sincere, upbeat) and your body language (cupping your chin in your hand can show serious consideration) to encourage your speaker to communicate what's really on his or her mind.

Don't judge. Does the speaker's body language, facial expressions, or tone of voice confirm or deny the message? If it does or you're not sure, ask. If you feel uncomfortable asking, describe what you think you heard.

See the speaker's point of view. You don't have to agree with what a person says to be a good listener, but you do have to take seriously what he or she has to say. Nodding your head and punctuating your speaker's message with comments such as "I see," and "I hadn't realized that" encourage speakers to continue. And who can tell? The speaker may be right. You might learn something new. If you don't give the speaker a chance, you'll never know.

Listen with your mind. To evaluate the "why" as well as the "what" of any message, separate your intellect from your emotions. In other words, keep an open mind.

If you feel a speaker pressing too heavily on one of your cherished "hotbuttons," do all you can to prevent yourself from interrupting. This gives you time to calm down, think of a more effective response, and keep from saying something you might later regret. It also allows the speaker to finish what he or she has to say.

Allowing your speaker to continue also creates an opportunity for you to change your mind or gather more ammunition for your response.

To Determine

Don't let your emotions get in the way of your message. You want to have all the information you need to make the best decision as to how to respond. Interrupting a speaker, mentally blocking anything you don't agree with, or forming an opinion before the speaker has delivered the message undermines the whole process of communication. Listening doesn't mean agreeing; it means listening.

Control those "hotbuttons." We all have hotbuttons (subjects that just set us on fire). Some of these hotbuttons are positive and some are negative. Both can be disastrous. Unless you can control your hotbuttons (not interrupting is the first, big, and most difficult step), you can easily be controlled by them. A speaker who knows your hotbuttons, for example, can manipulate you to act in ways you might later regret.

Don't jump to conclusions. Even a favorable conclusion can do a disservice to you and your speaker if it is not carefully thought out. Hiring someone too soon after an interview, for example, may not be in anyone's best interest and a waste of time, money, and energy for everyone concerned.

Decide how you're going to respond. But don't prepare your response until you're certain your speaker is very near the end of his or her message. Make sure your first response is positive. Even if you disagree with everything the speaker says, you can acknowledge the time and effort the speaker made to talk with you.

To Reply

Open with a positive. You're already responding positively when you don't interrupt a speaker, maintain a listening posture, and send verbal as well as nonverbal affirmations. To keep your hot streak going:

Rephrase and repeat. To repeat a speaker's message in your own words shows you've been listening and gives the speaker an opportunity to correct any misunderstanding.

Ask questions of clarification. Not only does the speaker have another opportunity to make his or her point, you have another opportunity to know for sure what's on the speaker's mind.

Admit when they're right. Admit they're right even when they are critical of you, then accept responsibility for whatever offense you may have committed and assure the speaker it won't happen again.

Ask for time. For any criticism you disagree with, ask for some time to think about what the speaker has said. This gives both of you a chance to calm down, provides you with some time to respond more thoughtfully, and gives the speaker a similar opportunity to be more objective. When you do reply, he or she should be more receptive to your point of view. Especially after you've set it up with all the positives of not interrupting, asking questions to make sure of what the speaker means, and admitting when you've made a mistake.

Watch your body language. You don't want to say with a frown on your face how much you appreciate someone's complaint. This is not to say you should respond cheerfully to criticism either; rather, it is to say that you want to appear open and receptive to what people have to tell you.

Focus on the issue or the content. Respond to the issues, not the person. Responding with "You're always . . ." or "Why can't you ever . . ." creates barriers rather than builds bridges. No one likes to be reminded of their negative history. Consider using "I" statements ("When I'm alone in the office, I get overwhelmed with . . .") and staying in the present ("What can we do now?") or the future ("If we can get this done in the next hour, we can . . .").

Consider not saying anything. Sometimes people just want you to listen.

16

How to Do Business over the Phone

There are two kinds of telephone calls: those we make and those we take. In both, a good first impression is crucial to our success and the success of the organization we represent. Consider making these tips work for you:

For the Calls We Take

Answer quickly. The sooner you answer the phone (within three rings is best), the sooner you please your callers. Impressed by your efficiency, they will more disposed to trust you to handle their needs quickly and efficiently.

Tell them your name. Even if they are too preoccupied with their own concerns to remember your name, your callers will appreciate the feeling of talking to a genuine human being rather than a company functionary.

Avoid the "hold" button. If you have to put some of your callers on hold, don't leave them there for more than 20 or 30 seconds without checking back on them. By telling them their call is important and what you plan to do to help them, you give your callers a sense of confidence and control. In other words, they're not left hanging.

Speak in your own natural voice. Always use an appropriate natural voice. Avoid slang or idiomatic expressions and rely on the words that have worked for you in the past. Your callers will be grateful they're not talking to an automaton, and you will appear confident and willing to help.

Listen. Listen to more than the words. They make up only 7 percent of any verbal conversation, and you can't see your callers' facial expressions or body language. You want to be especially sensitive to voice inflection, innuendo, and possible hidden agendas, but you can't do this effectively while addressing envelopes, filing folders, or talking to someone at the desk next to yours.

Give your callers your individual attention. They can tell when you're distracted and, even though you may get their words right, you run a great risk of missing the telling tone of voice they're using to convey those words.

Take notes. Write down any caller's name and use it in the conversation that follows. If you're forwarding a message, consider noting the caller's mood.

Provide positive feedback. Punctuating your callers' statements with affirmations such as "Yes," "I see," and "I understand" show your concern, ability to empathize, and willingness to help.

Don't interrupt. Your impatience will be seen as a measurement of how your company treats its clients, colleagues, and customers. If a caller is especially long-winded and you have no choice but to interrupt, ask a question that will help identify the direction the caller wants to go in. Long-winded people don't mind interruptions if they can continue to talk about themselves.

Don't jump to conclusions. Allow your callers to say what's on their minds. If you respond too quickly to what you think are their needs or transfer them to someone who can't help them, you'll come off as either stupid or careless.

Smile. Your callers can't see you, but they can tell when you enjoy helping them. So let them feel how much pleasure it gives you to satisfy their needs. The impression you make will last longer than anything you say.

For the Calls We Make

Be prepared. Know as much as you can about the people you call and the companies they work for. The more you know, the more ways you have of influencing them.

Also know what you want to say. And, if it's a product, service, or an idea you want to discuss, believe in it. This gives you the confidence and positive attitude you need to make your conversation a success. Realize, however, that your control of your listener's mood or circumstances is limited. Don't take any rejections personally.

Be assertive. "Mary Walsh, please" can be more effective than "Is Ms. Walsh in?" because it conveys a sense of control and importance. On the other hand, "This is John Tichenor from Fax International. May I speak to Mary Walsh?" is polite and often more effective because it denotes greater respect and consideration for your first listener.

State your name and the company you represent. You'll probably be asked anyway, so give your name and keep as much control over the conversation as you can for as long as you can.

Be friendly. If the person you're speaking with is screening your call, you need that person on your side. Acting put out or insulted by having to jump through a few hoops isn't going to get you where you want to be. Even if you don't get through, you establish a contact and begin laying the foundation for future calls.

Ask questions. Even the most experienced screener appreciates being treated like a human being. Asking open-ended questions shows that someone is interested in them as well as getting past them. Questions also can help you gain the information you need to make your target conversation a success.

If your screener replies to your open-ended questions with mostly monosyllabic statements (e.g., "Yes," "No," "Maybe"), don't push further. Politely bring the conversation to a close and continue your search for someone who is more receptive.

Listen. Listen to more than the words. In most cases, the tone of voice is more important. If the tone is negative (e.g., curt, impatient, irritated), show that you are someone who's easy to get along with: "If this is a bad time, I can get back to you tomorrow morning or later this week." You remain in control, you provide alternatives that are in your best interests, you keep open the possibility of a future conversation, and you impress your listener as someone who is sensitive to the needs of others.

Provide alternatives. Dr. Spock has been telling us for years not to tell children they have to eat their vegetables. The more effective way is to give them a choice: "Broccoli or string beans, George." The same technique works for your listeners because it gives them the sense of being in control, and choosing between alternatives is easier than having to think of something to say or do. If, for example, the person you want to speak with is unavailable, ask if 3 o'clock this afternoon or

10 o'clock the next morning is more convenient. Chances are your listener will either choose one of these times or suggestive an alternative.

And Now for the Tough Calls

Two you take (the screened call and the customer service call) and one you make (the sales call). All are difficult because they involve the risks, fears, and the consequences of rejection.

Screening Calls

Screening calls is no fun, but helping people can be. So instead of thinking of yourself as a resented barrier to your callers (which is how they see you), see yourself as a service representative. When you ask your callers for their names and the names of the companies they represent and they resist because they fear you'll block their calls, tell them you need to know to help them get through. With this approach, you're on your callers' side as well as that of your company.

A second approach to servicing rather than merely screening is to take statements often interpreted by callers as a "brush off" or "runaround" and turn them into opportunities to be helpful. When, for example, you say your boss is in a meeting, your callers often hear this as an excuse for not putting their call through. You can reverse this impression by telling a caller, "Ms. Walsh is in a meeting right now. Is there a time this afternoon when she can call you?"

Here's another opportunity for you to be helpful. Say your caller wants to talk to Ms. Walsh and Ms. Walsh isn't back from lunch. Instead of telling your caller Ms. Walsh is still at lunch (read: Ms. Walsh takes long lunches), tell your caller that you expect Ms. Walsh to be back from her appointment before 2:30 and offer to have her return your listener's call before 3:00.

The easiest way to turn negatively perceived statements into positive ones, however, is to ask, "How can I help you?" Use your caller's name; that shows your personal willingness to help in ways that go beyond those of a mere functionary.

The Customer Service Call

These calls are especially difficult because so many of them are complaints. Rarely does someone call the customer service department of any organization to say what a good job the company is doing. Here are some ways to handle angry callers:

Keep breathing. It isn't easy listening to what angry callers have to say, and their aggressive tone can depress you if you take them personally. Remember, they're not angry at you, they're just taking out their anger on you.

Relax, stay calm, or at least give the impression of being calm. When you remain calm, you create the image in your caller's mind of someone who is confident and experienced.

Keep them talking. Let your callers get as much of their anger out of their systems as they can before you respond. Encourage them to say more than they hoped to with sympathetic statements such as "I understand," "That's terrible," "That never should have happened," and "You must feel awful."

Ask questions. Questions give your callers another opportunity to vent their anger, but questions also provide them and you with further opportunities to discover the best ways to handle any problem.

Be on their side. Even if your callers are wrong, your first responses should be sympathetic. You don't have to accept responsibility for anything that happened. Instead of saying, for example, "I'm sorry you got sick in our restaurant," you can say "I'm sorry you got sick." The more sympathetic you can be, the more receptive your callers will be to whatever you suggest later. Call them by name (it's hard to be angry with someone who does this) and describe in your own words what they experienced. Thank them for bringing this matter to your company's attention.

Slip in the negative. This is known as the "Sandwich Technique":

- Say something positive.
- Slip in the negative.
- Say something positive.

You've already listened, asked questions, and responded sympathetically. In short, you've set your caller up for any bad news. State what you need to say clearly and firmly so there are no mistakes and no false hopes. Then quickly move on to something positive.

Offer to compensate. Even if your callers are totally off base, explain why your company is not responsible and offer some compensation: a free voucher, for example, or a 10 percent discount on any future purchase. This way your caller doesn't lose; he or she at least gets off the phone with something and may be willing to give your company another chance based on the way you responded.

The Sales Call

The toughest of them all is the sales calll because few people you call know of any reason why they should want to speak with you. To increase your chances of success on the phone:

Prepare. Knowing what you sell, whether it be a product, service, or an idea, is a great confidence builder. Especially if you believe that what you're selling helps people meet their needs.

Knowing your prospective customers and the companies they work for also boosts confidence, in you as well as in them. The more you know about a company's needs and goals, the more ways you have of influencing any decision.

Call. State your name and company before being asked, and be friendly to whomever picks up the phone. If your first listener is someone whose job is to screen calls, ask for their help. You have something that is really going to make life better for everyone at the company, and you don't want them to miss an opportunity to learn about it. If the person you want isn't available, can your screener suggest someone you could talk with?

The important thing here is to try to keep your listener from saying "no." The longer you can delay a "no," the better your chances of getting another "yes." Look, for example, at this script:

- "Hello. My name is John Tichenor from Fax International. Would you help me?" (This is not a question many people can say "no" to.)
- "If I can."
- "Usually I would speak to the person in charge of telecommunications in your company. Can you tell me who that is?"
- "Mary Walsh."
- "Could you connect me with Ms. Walsh?"

You might get a "no" here, but your chances of being put through to Ms. Walsh have been increased by your ability to keep your listener from hitting you with a "no" shortly after you started talking.

Listen. Any successful salesperson will tell you that you sell more by listening than by anything else. Put yourself in the position of someone who can meet their needs. To help them in the best ways that you can, they need to tell you all they can about their problems, and you need to hear it to help them make the decisions that are best for their company. So, if you're going to say anything, ask open-ended questions about the business. The more you can get your prospective customers to talk, the smarter they'll think you are. And you'll confirm their impression by tailoring your responses to the information they give you.

Think. Put yourself in your prospective clients' shoes. See as much as you can from their points of view. Ask yourself, "What's in this for them?" "How will they benefit?"

Present. The most important thing in presenting is to get your prospective customer to agree with you. So begin by summarizing in your own words the problems you've been listening to. Maybe you detected a "hotbutton" you can press and satisfy (logic isn't always the most effective selling tool). Start with your customer's most important need. Pretend you're a buyer for the company and you're trying to convince a supervisor to take a close look at something you know will benefit the company.

Expect objections. Few sales take place without objections, and everything you've done up to this point should give you most of what you need to handle any objections effectively. Your first response to objections should be to remain calm. You don't want to blow everything you've worked so hard for by acting defensive or allowing your emotions to get the best of you.

An effective second response is to answer the objection. If you think the objection is an excuse to bring the conversation to a close, ask a question about your customer's needs. This gives you another opportunity to tailor the benefits of your product, service, or idea to his or her needs. Be practical, realistic, and focused on the company's problems first and the benefits of whatever you're selling second.

The most common objection is price so, unless you're selling directly over the phone, you want to avoid price. You want an appointment. Selling 15 minutes is easier than selling just about anything that costs money. An effective close for an appointment could be something like this:

"I'm meeting with someone at NFC in your building this Thursday at 10 a.m. How would you like to meet at 9:00, or is later in the afternoon better for you?"

If you are selling over the phone and you're told the price is too high, here are some ways to respond:

Agree. "It is high. Or at least many customers thought it was high until they saw how much time and money it saved them. What are you spending now on . . . ?"

Agree. "It is high. But how much more time and money will your company spend if you don't implement what I'm offering? What are you spending now on . . . ?"

Agree. "It is high. But we guarantee everything we sell. Compare our warranty with that of any other competitor. What are you spending now on . . . ?"

Agree. "It is high. But you get what you pay for. To provide this quality costs more, but you will save more. Within three years, this product will have paid for itself just on the savings you'll reap. Let's take a look at the overall package. What are you spending now on . . . ?"

Agree. "It is high. But not as high as the cost of doing business without this product. Let's take a look at the overall package. What are you spending now on . . . ?"

Close. There are many ways to close a sales presentation, but there is only one person who can determine which one to use and when to implement it: the prospective customer.

Some of the signals a prospective client might send include silence (you've answered all their questions), shifting to the features rather than the benefits ("What colors does this come in?"), and asking questions about how soon your product, service, or idea can be implemented.

An effective response to these signals depends on what you've learned from talking with your prospective client. "Shall I order one for you?" may be best with a straightforward type of person, while shifting to the products' features will help a less confident buyer ("Do you want the red or the blue?"). Reviewing the benefits as they pertain to your customer's needs helps reinforce what should be going on in his or her mind, and asking your clients if they'd like some more time to think before making a decision shows consideration for their feelings and respect for their intelligence.

Tip: Once you've made your closing statement, try not to say anything more. Let the pressure of your silence bring its full force to bear on your prospective client. To talk further at this point only lets them off the hook. If you're forced to say something, however, consider going right to the heart of the matter: "You seem hesitant, Ms. Walsh. Tell me what's troubling you. Perhaps I can help."

17

How to Create Effective Presentations

R.H. Bruskin Associates twice conducted a national survey on what people fear most. Height, insects, lack of money, deep water, sickness, flying, loneliness, and even death came in distant seconds to speaking before a group.

To reduce your fear of public speaking and triumph over every audience and subject:

Be prepared. Know what you're talking about and know who you're speaking to. It's as simple and as complex as that. To be prepared:

Know your subject. If you know your subject (and you don't have to know much about any subject to know a lot more than many other people), you don't have to worry about what you don't know. You can focus on sharing with your audience what you know will help .them. If someone does ask you a question about something you're not sure of, say, "I'm not sure." You will be respected for your honesty. To be appreciated for your resourcefulness as well, add, "But I'll find out for you" or "Does anyone in the audience have a solution to this problem?" You'll be amazed at how many hands go up if the members of your audience are from the same field.

And don't be embarrassed. You can't know everything (no one expects you to), and now you have an opportunity to not only learn something new but also to create a learning experience for at least one member of your audience if not more. If something you said raised a question in one person's mind, chances are several others had the same question but didn't ask it because they didn't want to focus everybody's attention on what they thought was their own problem.

Know your audience. Because of the topic of your presentation, most of the people in your audience will probably come from similar backgrounds: business, industry, education, the military, health, religion, and the like. Chances are, because you're speaking to them, you share their interests and concerns. And they've come to get your help in improving their lives in some way: to sell more, produce faster, cut costs, manage better, and so on. In short, to be more effective at what they do. Because you have so much in common, you have all the clues you need to know what's important to them. So ask yourself:

- What makes me/them tick?
- What motivates me/them?
- What gets me/them excited?
- What is my/their greatest fear?
- What is it that sets me/them on fire?

Your answers are what you want to talk about; they are the topics your audience wants you to address.

Cluster. Remember the clustering exercise you learned as a writing technique (pp. 65) and as a memory device (pp. 78)? It can also be used to brainmap presentations. If, for example, I was going to give a speech (or write a chapter in a book) on how to create effective presentations, my cluster might (and it did) look something like this:

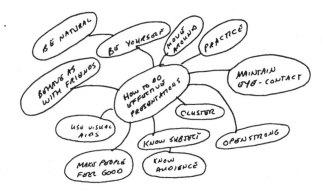

My outline would then be:

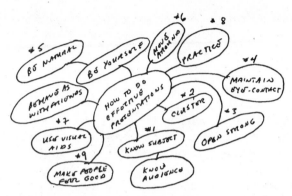

To follow these points more easily while giving my speech, I would place
my outline in a linear form:

- Know your subject; know your audience.
- Cluster your thoughts.
- Open strong.
- Maintain eye contact.
- Be yourself; be natural; behave as you would with friends.
- Move around.
- Use visual aids.
- Practice.
- Make people feel good.

I might try to memorize the order of my list, but more likely, when I
speak, I'd keep it someplace where I could refer to it when I needed to.
Knowing what I'm going to say about each point, I'd just have to see
each point as a subject heading. Each subject heading would serve as a
trigger for my memory and would keep my mind close to the theme of
my presentation.

Open strong. A good beginning is as important to a presentation as a
powerful opening sentence is to anything you write. The opening
determines whether your audience wants to hear more. Most of the
people in most audiences will decide this in the first 90 seconds of your
speech. Here are some effective openings for speeches as well as for
anything you write:

An acknowledgment. It doesn't hurt to tell the people who invited you
and are eager to hear what you have to say how happy you are to have
such a wonderful opportunity.

An anecdote. The most effective anecdote is a story that says something about yourself, is relevant to your audience's interests, and lays the foundation on which your speech is built.

A joke. The joke, the most common of openings, is successful because it puts people at ease; it can be unsuccessful because opening jokes are so overdone. If you're going to open with a joke, make sure it's a good one and it's relevant to what you're going to talk about.

A startling fact. You have a better chance of getting shot in the United States on any given day than you have of winning any state lottery. This is a startling fact. Over 20,000 Americans die each year from handguns. In Great Britain, 20 die from handguns; in Sweden, the number is 8. The image created by the first fact, followed up by the statistics of the second grip the audience's imagination and should make them want to hear more.

A question. The advantage of a question (rhetorical or not) is that you have your audience participating in your speech right from the first sentence. Asking questions that require a show of hands has the audience participating without the risk of someone raising his or her hand and going on about a problem that is of little interest to many others. When someone does answer your question, repeat the answer to the audience before commenting on it. If the person responding talks at length, don't interrupt. Sum up the response and move on but shorten the length of time you left for audience responses.

Establish eye contact. Many books on public speaking encourage readers to focus their eyes on wall objects behind their audiences. This technique is supposed to alleviate panic but, as anyone who has ever tried it knows, it only increases panic. Nothing you say sounds natural, you become increasingly self-conscious about what you're saying and doing, and your audience responds the same way you would if someone speaking to you addressed every word to some object on a wall.

Be yourself. One of the worst things a speaker can do is try to look and sound like he or she thinks a speaker should look and sound. Think of George Bush as an example of this kind of speaker. Many of Bush's presentations seemed artificial and contributed to his reputation for being "out of touch."

Now compare George Bush's speaking style (not his politics) with those of his successor. Bill Clinton's voice has a much wider range of inflection and tone, his hands don't grip any lectern (they reach out to the people beyond it), tears on occasion will well in his eyes and, when he smiles, there's never a sense that his smile discomforts him in any way.

This is not to say that you should be yourself to the point that you want to use slang or certain idiomatic expressions— though you can if you do it ironically or in a way that calls special attention to the words your're using. Rather, you should speak in your own natural voice and use the same words and gestures you would use if you were standing before a small group of people in your living room and expressing your views on something you feel strongly about. In other words, you are you regardless of whether you're speaking to 4 or 400 people.

Move around. If you can get off a podium or out from behind any lectern, do it. All they do in most cases is create a barrier between you and your audience. Let your audience see you in all your glory. Get as close to them as you can. Walk back and forth across the front of the room and up and down the aisles.

Pacing will also help you relieve any anxiety you might have about speaking but be careful: too much pacing makes you seem nervous.

Use visual aids. People like to see pictures. Very often we'll remember a story we've heard longer than we'll remember the point of a story. Why? Because the mental picture created by the story grabs the stronger hold on our imaginations. And when we do remember the lesson, the reason almost always is that we've remembered the story that goes with it.

Stories are visual aids because they create mental pictures in your listeners' minds. So don't overuse them. Not every point has to be reinforced with a story.

And for the visual aids that don't ask your listeners to imagine (overhead transparencies, slide projections, blackboard diagrams, flow-top graphs) consider these suggestions:

Don't use too many. People won't be able to keep track of them and will tire of looking at them.

Use aids that form pictures. Graphs, pictures, illustrations, tables, and whatever else you consider using should provide your audience with a point or insight that would require more words to explain than you have time for.

Don't data dump. More than one idea to a visual or more than one visual to an illustration can distract an audience.

Check the back row. Make sure your visuals are big enough for everyone to see. And make them look good. Consider color combinations and opt for clarity over clutter. If you use a pointer, point at the screen, not at the overhead projector. When you point at the projector, you risk blocking somebody's view of the screen.

Note: You are a visual aid. Don't distract from your message by wearing clothes that are too loud, too bright, or clash.

Practice. Rehearse your speech, time it, and then, when you really have it down, present it to a group of friends. Live bodies make for a far more realistic experience, and you have the added benefit of some immediate feedback when you're through. If your speech is too long, cut some of it out. Don't plan to speak faster.

Make people feel good. The people in your audience want to learn something and they want to have a good time doing it. So don't be critical of any profession without balancing your criticism with credits, don't put down any city you're speaking in (especially Cleveland and Buffalo), don't joke about people from any specific age, race, ethnic, or religious group, and don't touch anyone in the audience (it invades the private space of the person you touch and sends signals you can't control all over the room). Instead, focus on how you can help the members of your audience be better at what they do.

Any Questions?

What I've written in this chapter is pretty close to the outline I created, and a few things came to mind in the writing that I hadn't thought of when I created my cluster but, if you don't have any questions at this point, I've failed. That's what no questions at the end of a speech means: You failed. Either you've talked too much, said too little, offended too many, didn't convince enough, or got so wrapped up in what you were talking about that no one understood what you were saying.

If I've done a successful job so far in this chapter, there should be some questions in your mind. Questions such as:

Q. What if I know everything I need to know about my subject and my audience and I'm still nervous?

A. Maybe you only think you know enough. See if there's more you can learn. The more you learn and practice what you want to say, the less anxious you should become. Also, it's important to note that a little nervousness is good for a speaker. It helps keep him or her alert and contributes to the intensity all speakers need to make their audiences realize the importance and urgency of the message. The trick is to get all those butterflies in your stomach to fly in the same direction. Knowledge, conviction, and intensity help you do that.

Q. Isn't it true that some speakers are just more talented than others?

A. Yes, but public speaking is also a skill. Whatever your natural ability as a communicator, raising your skill level will improve on that ability. If you can swing a tennis racquet or ski down a hill without falling, you can speak better in public. You may never be the Martina Navratilova of public speakers (unless, of course, you put the same time and energy into your speaking ability that Martina Navratilova puts into her profession), but you can and will be competent. Then you, too, will be a household name.

Q. You talked about getting out from behind the lectern, but how can anyone hear you after you leave the microphone?

A. Wear a lavalier (named after the pendants worn by the Duchess de La Valliere, the famous mistress of Louis XIV). And here's another reason for leaving the lectern: most lecterns are used to promote a hotel or organization. Picture someone standing behind an advertisement, reading a speech, and using their hands for little more than turning pages. Does this person have anything to say to you?

18

How to Make Every Meeting Worthwhile

Before holding any meeting, ask yourself: Is this meeting necessary? Very often meetings are held for no other than two reasons (1) they're scheduled to be held, or (2) the time since the last meeting has grown to more than a month.

To conduct meetings that people look forward to attending, enjoy participating in, and leave with the feeling of having accomplished something, consider these suggestions:

Prepare. Two hours of preparation for every one hour of meeting is a reasonable guideline. The more thoroughly you plan your meeting, the more organized and efficient it will be. Use your cluster technique to determine: the purpose of the meeting, who should attend, where it should be held, what topics it should include, what you want to say about them, when it should begin, how long it should last, and how much time should be allocated for each item on your agenda.

The agenda, which should be distributed to the meeting's participants anywhere from 48 hours to a week in advance, separates the professional meeting planner from the amateur. The professional agenda, written on a single piece of paper, states the times and location of the meeting, its specific purpose, the topics to be discussed, the names of those presenting reports, the resources or supplies the participants should bring, and some built-in but unmentioned time for the unexpected.

The best planners choose a time (an hour before lunch helps people stick to the agenda) and a place (better to cancel a meeting or move it to another location if an on-site room isn't available or is unsuitable). The best planners also check their rooms before any meeting. Is it too hot (people will doze) or too cool (people will be distracted)? Is it too dark? (Darker rooms depress people's energy levels.) Is it clean? (Untidy rooms put people in negative moods.) Are the chairs properly arranged? (A circle encourages discussion.) Are there tables for taking notes? Is there a blackboard, flow-top chart, or overhead projector (check the spare bulb) available for relaying information or brainstorming a project?

Inform. Accompanying the agenda you distribute prior to a meeting should be an announcement of the meeting's time and place, it's purpose, and what you expect from the participants. You may, for example, ask the participants to write their opinions of the topics to be discussed (this forces them to take the issues more seriously), or you might ask each participant to complete a survey in time for you to tabulate the responses and bring them to the meeting.

Lead. There are all kinds of leaders. Here are what separates the good and the best.

The Good Leaders	vs.	The Best Leaders
Begin on time to be fair to the people who are there.		Begin on time and don't fill in latecomers on what they've missed.
Keep the meeting on track.		Ask a participant to serve as gatekeeper. The gatekeeper's job is to interrupt anyone who digresses from the meeting's agenda.
Answer questions and resolve problems.		Answer some questions and make every problem a group issue.
Respond directly to complaints and challenges.		Ask other members of the group to respond to an opinion or thrust the responsibility of meeting the challenge back to the person who made it (e.g., "Good point, John. What do you think we should do about it?").
Remind troublesome participants of their responsibilities at meetings.		Focus on the issue not the person.
Give everyone a chance to speak (e.g., "Any questions before we move on?").		Make sure everyone has contributed (e.g., "Mary, what do you think of John's suggestion?").

Try to get people to agree.	Search for a consensus. They know it's more important that everybody understand and support a decision even if they don't agree with it.
End the meeting on time (they know that people have work to do).	End the meeting early (they know that busy people appreciate extra time).

Participate. The best meeting members are future best leaders. They separate themselves from the rest by:

- Doing their homework (even to the point of reviewing the last meeting's minutes).
- Thinking about and writing down the points they want to see addressed.
- Arriving on time.
- Sitting in different places and next to different people.
- Listening with an open mind to what everyone has to say.
- Not interrupting anyone.
- Not jumping to conclusions.
- Not whispering to someone while someone else is talking.
- Saving their comments until everyone else has given theirs.
- Taking notes.
- Asking questions that keep the meeting on track.

Record. The best device for brainstorming any subject and recording any opinion is the cluster (see pp. 32). The person chosen to create the cluster stands at a blackboard, flow-top chart, or overhead projector and creates a cluster of all the thoughts of all the people in the group. No idea is censured, every suggestion is recorded, and no opinion is discussed until all the contributions are recorded. Once the participants can see their thoughts all at once in the cluster, they can evaluate which ones are good, which ones not so good, which ones they want to try first, second, third, and so on.

Review. You know your meeting was a success when it satisfied these criteria:

- It began and ended on time.
- There was some quality in the work done.

- Something was accomplished (other than beginning and ending on time).
- Everyone felt as if their time had been well spent; no one thought he or she wasted time.

To make sure your meeting was a success, ask the opinion of the participants. Consider a "Mostly agree," "Partly agree," "Partly disagree," "Mostly disagree" evaluation form with room at the end for written comments.

Here are some statements you might want to present on an evaluation form:

- The purpose of the meeting was clearly stated and adhered to.
- The meeting's leader came prepared to lead discussions of the items on the agenda.
- The participants were prepared to discuss the items on the agenda.
- The time allocated for each topic was satisfactory.
- There was enough time to hear everyone's opinion.
- The leader kept the participants focused on what was important.
- Everyone was given an opportunity to contribute.
- The topics discussed were relevant.
- Everyone understood what was expected of them.
- All the presenters were thoroughly prepared.
- No ideas were dismissed; all were taken seriously and recorded equally.
- Decisions were reached by consensus rather than by someone's predetermined conclusion.

Add your relevant statements to these and distribute copies of your evaluation to the participants at the end of the meeting. Ask that the evaluation forms be completed and returned to you by the end of the day or by 10 a.m. the following morning. Be specific about the time and place to insure you'll receive them.

Follow up. If minutes have been taken during the meeting, have them written up and distributed to the participants within 24 hours of the meeting. Record and distribute the results of the participants' evaluations within 24 hours of their having submitted them. Note what went well (and plan to repeat it) and what didn't go so well (and learn from your mistakes). Then think of anything you can do to make your next meeting even more successful:

- Invite a guest speaker.
- Order pizza or hold the meeting in a private room of a restaurant.
- Rotate the position of gatekeeper and leader with each meeting.
- Show a training video.
- Use a round table.
- Don't take everything so seriously. Ask what can I do to make my next meeting more fun?

19

How to Negotiate Win-Win Situations

Successful negotiators know that winning isn't the only thing. They see conflict as an opportunity for understanding and growth, believe compromise is more effective than victory. Successful negotiators are patient, are sensitive to others' needs, are not overly bothered when personally attacked, and always have the Right Attitude: commitment to a win-win solution.

In a win-win solution, every party in the negotiating process gets something they need. Few get all they want, but no one is left empty-handed. Not everyone is totally happy with the solution but, because everyone has something to gain from it, everyone will work to make the solution a success. And the success of any win-win solution encourages the negotiators to work together again to develop more successful solutions.

The secret of reaching win-win solutions is to focus on how to meet the needs of each party in the negotiation; in other words, to put yourself in the shoes of each person you negotiate with and see the problem from his or her point of view.

To reach a win-win solution in any negotiation, follow these strategies:

Know. Most people know what they want out of any negotiation, but few consider what they're willing to give up for it.

And what about the other party's objectives? Learn what you can about the other's position; then evaluate that information in a solution that benefits everyone.

Define. Understand thoroughly and be able to explain clearly the issues as you see them. What reasons do you have to justify your position? How will you present your reasons so the other party will understand them from your point of view? What will the other party think of your viewpoint? What will be their arguments against your position? On what points will they be accurate and how will you respond?

Separate needs from wants. Negotiating a win-win solution means giving up some thing(s) you want to get some thing(s) you need. So know before entering any negotiation how much you can afford to lose. Also know what alternatives you will turn to if your minimum requirements aren't satisfied.

Meet. Many inexperienced negotiators fail to reach a solution before they begin to negotiate because they see the other person as "the enemy." Thinking of the other negotiator as an opponent reduces the negotiating process to a win-lose contest which, in turn, portrays anyone holding a different viewpoint as either stupid or evil.

Successful negotiators take whatever time they can to get to know the people they will be negotiating with. They know if they can establish a rapport with someone, they can communicate more easily and identify more accurately the common interests necessary for creating a win-win solution.

So don't wait until it's time to negotiate to build a rapport. Ask to meet beforehand with your negotiator. Perhaps you can have breakfast the morning of your meeting. Or dinner the night before. Explain to the other party that you don't want to discuss any of the issues for negotiation; you just want to get to know him or her. If the person is skeptical, point out that your objective in the upcoming negotiation is to reach a resolution that meets everyone's needs; meeting beforehand might help establish a climate for easier communication once the negotiations begin.

State the issues. This is a common first step in any negotiation because it gives each party an opportunity to present their view of the problem. The closer the parties can come to agreeing on a definition of the problem, the easier it will be for them to negotiate a solution. In fact, reaching a solution is relatively easy if both parties believe they've accurately defined the problem.

Listen. Pay careful attention to the words, the nuances, the inflections, the tones of voice. Does the other party repeat any points? Does he or she introduce issues not covered in the definition of the problem? Knowing why these issues are important can help you negotiate more effectively later on.

Observe. Is the negotiator's body language at variance with the spoken message or agreed-to definition of the problem? Does the other person frown or appear open-minded? Does he or she perspire or appear relaxed? Are the arms and legs crossed in a comfortable or resistant way? Do the hand gestures indicate passion, anger, or indifference? Knowing what's really at issue for the negotiator provides you with bargaining chips that you can play later on.

Present. Say what you want but present it in terms that support the definition of the issue you and the other party already agreed on. Show how your solution benefits the needs of both parties. Focus on the present and the future; bringing up unpleasant history will only cause division. If you do mention the past, show how your solution or a similar one has worked for others.

Listen again. Many negotiators, having said what they want, listen mostly for the points relevant to their side of the negotiation. You want to go one step further. You listen for what the other party really needs so you can decide if you are able to provide it.

Present again. Rephrase in your own words what you understand to be the other party's needs. If necessary, ask questions to further clarify any misconceptions you might have. Very often, the more your negotiator talks, the more he or she will respect you. Then, when you do speak, empathize with your negotiator's needs. Present your position from the point of view of what he or she has to gain.

If the other person hesitates, shift your focus to less critical issues or areas where you can easily agree. Build on these blocks of agreement toward a solution. Don't be afraid to drop an issue (you can always return to it later), and don't be afraid to change your position, redefine the issue, or suggest a new level of compromise. The important thing is to keep negotiating, to continue to search for areas of agreement. If nothing you try seems to work, ask the other party what he or she needs to reach a solution. Then synthesize your negotiator's reply into what you've already agreed on and show where his or her needs are or can be met.

Don't blow it. As heated as negotiations may become, they are always delicate, and one false move can undermine the whole process.

- Never resort to intimidating behavior (you'll undermine whatever strength your argument has).
- Never lose your patience (you'll appear as desperate).
- Never lose your temper (you'll be seen as uncooperative).
- Never say more than you need to say (you'll be suspected of not listening).
- Never issue an ultimatum (you'll create a win-lose situation).
- Never raise your voice (people don't hear well when others shout).

Successful negotiators try to get what they want, but they know that no negotiation is successful without some give and take. Rarely is compromise unnecessary. To put yourself into a noncompromising position is to create a lose-lose outcome. Not only do negotiators to get what they want, they also fail to, get what they need.

Successful negotiation isn't about power. It's about appreciating and acknowledging the differences between people and their varying points of view. The skill in negotiation comes from knowing what, when, and how much to give as well as what, when, and how much to expect in return. Give from what you want; hold out for what you need.

Part 4

Managing Yourself

The most important decision you make is to be
in a good mood.

VOLTAIRE

20

How to Manage Stress

There are two kinds of stress: the stress that is good for you and the stress that is bad for you. Good stress is when you're excited about something. Your heart rate increases, your blood pressure rises slightly, adrenaline is released in your body, and you take slightly shorter breaths of air. Bad stress creates the same physical effects only this time your body's responses work against you. Continued bad stress from such things as financial insecurity, an insensitive boss or supervisor, the inability to complete a project, or any such combination can lead to anger, frustration, fatigue, depression, headaches, hypertension, insomnia, inability to concentrate, indigestion, compulsive eating, ulcers, rapid mood swings, sexual dysfunction, high blood pressure, stroke, heart attack, substance abuse, a chronic inability of the immune system to fight common colds and viruses, even spouse and child abuse.

Getting Ahead! Career Skills That Work is a prescription for people who want to prevent work-related stress. Here's how to use it: Identify what causes your stress, look up the chapter corresponding to your problem, commit yourself to changing your current behavior, and start working immediately on developing the discipline you need to turn your commitment into a habit.

Some other ways to control your stress before it controls you include:

Having the Right Attitude. View the stressful situations in your life as opportunities or challenges. If you can meet these challenges, you can learn more about yourself, discover and practice the skills necessary to avoid repeating your harmful reactions to these stressful situations, gain greater control over your life, build the confidence you need to handle future pressures, and move out of any current ruts into the

113

minefield of deeper and wider ruts that await all of us no matter how well we prepare for them.

Prioritizing Don't try to do everything at once or too many things at the same time. Determining the order of what's important in your life prevents the random events of your life from becoming crises. Your list of priorities enables you to evaluate the worth of potentially stressful situations. Priorities seen as low or middle level will not create the same high level of stress as high-priority items.

To determine the time and energy you want to devote to any stress-inducing situation, ask to what extent the situation contributes to your long- and short-term goals. You'll be able to tolerate stress from your short-term goals (e.g., moody boss, office politics, lack of certain supplies) because you're aiming for something higher. Because you control the priorities, you also control the stress level of most tasks. When combined with an effective time management system (see pp. 22–31), priorities give you control over decisions, keep you on track toward your goals, provide you with the structure you need to determine how to approach daily tasks, and help you complete what's important.

Being flexible. Knowing your goals and prioritizing your tasks is important for reducing stress, but holding on too rigidly to these anchors can increase your stress level. The unexpected is inevitable. When it raises its ugly little head, confront it as a challenge for growth (as opposed to an agent of destruction) and adapt.

Don't fall into the trap of believing that your way of viewing a situation is necessarily the most accurate just because it's yours or your feel strongly about it. Avoid replaying the cliché-ridden mental tapes that no longer apply, shun the opportunity to blame others, and don't get hung up on how unfair life is. It's still better than death, and you have the power and ability to influence almost every situation you're in.

So use that power and ability. Strive to be objective, open-minded, and receptive to the views of others. Don't expect the behavior of others to be consistent and search for opportunities within crises to work on what you need to achieve the results you want.

Avoid transfering values. When you expect a person to act the same way you would in any given situation, you create in your mind a false image of that person. This is often called "putting a person down on a pedestal" because you don't see and accept the person as he or she really is but only as the image you've created. When that person doesn't behave the same way you would in the same circumstances, you're disappointed and your stress level rises with the frustration and possible anger that follows.

Be realistic in your expectations of others. Allow people to have their own values and experiences. Similarly, don't try to live up to the unrealistic expectations of others. Consider discussing your needs with these people to see if they are willing to acknowledge and accept them. If they're not, you're in a no-win situation.

Communicating. Focusing on a symptom of stress (a headache, for example) rather than the cause of that headache (tardy colleagues), and keeping the pressure created by the cause inside may provide short-term relief but only makes every situation worse and creates more stress for everyone. Instead of focusing on a symptom (e.g., headache), look at the symptom as a clue for identifying and correcting the cause (e.g., consistently late employees always give me a headache because they create an unfair burden on my time and energy).

Explain how you feel to those causing stress in your life: "When I'm alone in the office, I get overwhelmed with all the work and can't concentrate on what I was hired to do." Begin a dialogue on how to solve the problem: "On the days you come in late and I cover for you, will you cover for me on the days I have to leave early?"

Being objective. By keeping your long-term goals in sight and prioritizing what's important, you help maintain an overview of any situation. Monitoring that overview keeps you from getting bogged down with minor aggravations. You have more important things to do. When something unexpected does occur, your conscious decision to place it on your list of priorities prevents you from getting emotionally involved.

Accepting. Don't waste your time on what you can't change; focus on what you can. Look for opportunities to take you from the status quo to the new and more effective. Accepting what you can't influence doesn't mean giving up hope, however. It means temporarily directing your energy where you can make a difference.

To get through those situations where your control is minimal:

- Remind yourself that this situation, like many other unpleasant situations, will change.

- Recognize and accept the fact that you feel tense but don't let any negative feelings keep you down.

- Focus on tasks that contribute to your short- or long-term goals.

- Don't take offenses personally. The hostility or rudeness of others is their hostility or rudeness, not yours.

- Depend on yourself to see you through the hard times. Rescuers are a thing of the past.

- Do something nice for yourself: a dinner, a movie, a workout, a gift, whatever will make you feel better.

Breathe. In times of stress, you need to stop yourself from hopping on the anxiety bandwagon. So take a breath of air. Take a few of them. Sit in a comfortable position at your desk, close your eyes, and count to four. Give one second to each count: one, two, three, four. Then breathe in through your nose while counting to four. Try to fill your lungs with a little more air than is normally comfortable. Hold that air in your lungs for another count of four then, to a final four count, release the air through your mouth. You shouldn't have to do this more than a few times.

This method is more effective when combined with a visualization. Follow the breathing technique until you can visualize the successful outcome of your problem without stress. Then ask yourself what you did to reach that successful outcome. Your answer is your plan for action.

The advantage of combining the breathing exercise with a visualization is that it puts you in a state of relaxed concentration. This relaxed concentration state is your key to achievement. Through it you realize that you may want something (the successful outcome of your problem) but you're no longer so desperate that you're willing to do anything (even drive yourself crazy) to achieve it.

If you don't have time to breathe and visualize, tense every muscle in your body for 20 seconds; then release the tension. This won't solve any problem, but it will make you feel less tense about it.

Act. Identify the source of your aggravation, develop a strategy to combat the issue (not the person), and act. Don't allow yourself to be a victim of pressure, boredom, or the insensitive behavior of others. When you're always reacting, you're never in control of your life and, when you're always putting out fires or getting monkeys off your back, you're vulnerable.

Think about what you enjoy, what motivates you, what contributes to the completion of your long-term goals, and what gives you a sense of accomplishment. Then take the kind of action in those areas that will lead you to success and bring you the recognition you deserve.

Don't act. You don't have to act on every feeling. Consider accepting some of them (maybe you don't respond well to any kind of criticism), not judging them (feelings are neither right nor wrong, they just are), and choosing not to respond (sometimes we mistake "acting on" with "acting out;" the latter is almost always counterproductive). If you're going to act, think of your behavior in terms of what's more effective and less-effective rather than what's right or wrong.

Create closure. Note your accomplishments by crossing them off your to do list each time you complete a task, take a few seconds to sit back and relax before taking on a new assignment, keep your desk clear of anything not directly related to whatever you're working on, look back at what you accomplished at the end of each day, and leave your job at the office (where it belongs).

If you have to bring work home with you, set aside one time-block (9 to 10:30, for example) to do it. And don't work beyond the time you set for yourself unless your job is at stake. No job is worth sacrificing your life for.

Talk. If you waste any part of your day creating scenarios about what you should have said to whomever is currently causing stress in your life, you're contributing to your own stress level. And while you're getting all worked up, the person who offended you is getting work done, or eating or sleeping or playing golf. So why allow yourself to make things worse? Create a plan for the next time you have a confrontation with this person, act assertively when the time for confrontation comes (see pp. 119–123) and, in the meantime, let go of your frustration, anger, and pain by talking about how you feel with someone you trust, doing something you enjoy, working on what you can control, and resolving never to wrestle with pigs: you both get dirty and only the pig has a good time.

Prevent. A healthy lifestyle can help you reduce and better resist stress. Junk foods that are high in fat tire you because our body has to focus energy on digestion. Alcohol can offer some immediate relief to stress, but it can't cure the cause and can become a problem. Caffeine only increases anxiety. Stick to fresh fruit, raw vegetables, whole grains, and high-fiber roughage.

Regular exercise (e.g., an hour at a time, three days per week) not only reduces the immediate effects of stress (by limiting the flow of adrenaline induced by stress), it also strengthens your body's ability to combat stress (by increasing the amount of beta-morphins that your body needs to feel good). Most people discover they have more energy when they exercise regularly.

But don't over-exercise. Too much exercise causes an overproduction of cortisol, which is one of the anxiety-producing chemicals stress induces. At times when your stress level is high, consider following your exercise with a sauna bath or long, hot shower.

Get a good night's sleep. If stress keeps you awake at night, take power naps during the day. It may take some time and practice, but you can train yourself to take a 10-minute nap in a lounge or even at your desk. Not only do you awaken with renewed energy, your energy will often last well into the evening. Count on an extra hour of energy for every five minutes of power sleep.

Be good to yourself. Running yourself down, blaming yourself, assuming responsibility for the behavior of others, and imagining all the bad things that will happen (few do) only weakens the immune system. In times of stress, take time out. Go to a movie, have lunch with a friend, be with yourself for a while. You need it, you earned it, and you deserve it.

21

How to Assert Yourself

Assertion is more than a way of behaving; it's a state of mind. It's based on the principle that human beings have certain rights. Among these are the right to have opinions, the right to express views, the right to be responsible for your own behavior, the right to make a mistake, take a chance, change your mind, make a decision, judge yourself by your own standards, and say "yes" or "no" without feeling guilty.

Not to stand up for your rights is to reduce yourself to the level of a victim. Victims let others prevent them from expressing their wants and needs. Or they allow others to intimidate them to such an extent that any expression is so apologetic or self-demeaning that it can easily be disregarded as unimportant. Through their words and actions, victims send the message: You are more important than I; your thoughts are more serious than mine; your preferences deserve more respect; I don't amount to much; go ahead and take advantage of me. The payoff for victims is they avoid conflict and they rarely have to be responsible for their own behavior.

To protect your rights in ways that violate the rights of others is to reduce yourself to the level of a bully. Bullies, as we all know, are cowards pretending to be courageous. Afraid of losing control, they see challenge as a personal threat. Their response is to attack by humiliating, demeaning, or in some other way putting down the people whom they perceive as opponents. Bullies send this message: I'm okay and you're not; my way is right and your way is only your way; what I want is more important than what you need; anyone who disagrees with me is either stupid or evil. The payoff for bullies is they win. Or rather, they think they win. More often than not, they create real opponents who look for opportunities to sabotage the very areas of control the bullies fight so hard to protect.

When pressure comes to bear, it's easy to respond as a victim and it's easy to respond as a bully. What's hard is to walk the fine line that separates the two. To be compassionate without being weak and, at the same time, to be strong without becoming insensitive is the delicate balance known as "assertion."

Assertive behavior is honest, direct, and respectful of others' human rights. Its goal is the kind of win-win solutions that lead to greater trust, confidence, and cooperation among people.

To become more assertive:

Think positively. Assertive behavior begins inside of you. It's not just the way you act; it's who you are. If you're the kind of person who creates self-fulfilling prophecies from your own fear of failure, acting assertively will be just that: acting. Your words will sound like they came from a script and your behavior will look as awkward to others as if you put all your clothes on backwards.

Believe that though you may feel strongly about certain issues, you can change the ways you respond to these feelings. Changing the way you respond to a particular problem or person will present you with a different point of view of the problem or person. Use your imagination. Visualize saying and doing things successfully. The more powerful your mental image and the more positive your expectations, the greater and more frequent will be your successes.

Think of others. People will respond more favorably to your assertions if they believe you understand and take their position seriously. A colleague, for example, asks you to help complete a project, but you're worried about getting your own project done on time. You could agree to help your colleague and hope to complete your own project later and run the risk of making mistakes that you won't have time to correct (read: be a victim); you could tell your colleague to forget about getting help from you; you have your own problems to worry about (an aggressive rebuff that ensures you won't ever get any help from this person, unless he or she is a victim); or you could respond assertively (honestly and directly but with empathy for your colleague's position): "I'd gladly help you with your project if my own project wasn't so far from being completed on time." Another alternative is to suggest some way that the two of you could work together to get both projects in under the deadline wire.

Use "I" statements. Beginning a response with the word "I" enables you to express your feelings without attacking the other party. Compare, for example, these two statements:

- Do you have to smoke that now?

- I get sick when I have to breathe cigarette smoke. Could you please put it out or smoke somewhere else?

Most "I" statements are particularly effective because they don't judge the behavior of others as right or wrong, good or bad. They simply state the sender's preferences.

Time your assertion. If you need to confront a person:

Don't:

- Meet in a restaurant (too many distractions).

- Sit behind your desk (you want to build bridges not erect barriers).

Do:

- Avoid the end of the day (people are tired and want to go home).

- Sit or stand as the other person sits or stands (be an equal, not a towering bully or a cowering victim).

- Arrange your meeting when the person you need to talk to can give you the time and energy you both need to resolve the problem (before projects, after crises, a quiet hour of the day).

If you wish to assert yourself at a group meeting, give others a chance to speak first. The others' viewpoints will give you a sense of the group's position and provide you with clues as to how to best respond to whatever issue is being discussed.

Support your words. The words you say to protect your rights must be reinforced by your behavior. If your body language contradicts your spoken message, the people you're communicating with will pay more attention to the nonverbal message.

Consider the messages sent by these signals:

	Body Posture:	
Nonassertive	*Assertive*	*Aggressive*
Slumped shoulders. Head down; eyes averted.	Shoulders straight. Head erect but at ease.	Head erect but chin thrust forward. Eyes glaring.
	Hand Gestures:	
Nonassertive	*Assertive*	*Aggressive*
Hands at sides. Limp handshake. Constantly chewing on pen or pencil.	Relaxed hands. Open gestures. Firm handshake.	Clenched hands. No handshake or painful handshake. Directs people with pen or finger.

	Facial Expressions:	
Nonassertive	*Assertive*	*Aggressive*
Blinking eyes. Nervous smile. Lifted eyebrows.	Frequent eye contact. Sincere smile. Relaxed eyebrows.	Scowling eyes. Sarcastic smile. Furrowed brow.

	Tones of Voice:	
Nonassertive	*Assertive*	*Aggressive*
Apologetic, weak, imploring. Rises at the end of a sentence to turn every statement into a question. Nervous, self-concious laughter.	Objective, resonant, confident. Remains smooth, pleasant inflections. Laughter inspired by humor.	Angry, flippant, scornful. Pitch makes words sound like orders. Sarcastic laughter.

Note that the nonassertive messages all reveal the sender's fear or unwillingness to express his or her true preferences. Because these preferences are important enough to feel but not crucial enough to express, they're held within to eat away at the sender's desired self-image. The aggressive body signals, on the other hand, send the message that the sender's preferences are more important than those of anyone else. So important, in fact, that the sender will minimize the worth of anyone who feels or acts differently.

Balanced between these two extremes, the assertive person signals an open and honest expression of preferences that doesn't impinge on the rights of others.

Beware of mixed signals. Some aggressive people behave in ways that are passive, or seemingly passive. They withdraw to themselves and refuse to participate. These are the people who, when you notice something is wrong and ask them about it, reply: "Nothing's wrong" or "Forget about it; it's not your problem." What separates the passive aggressive from the merely passive, however, is the tone of voice. Instead of being timid and self-denying, the tone is sarcastic, scornful, condescending, challenging, and accompanied by many of the body signals usually associated with the aggressive personality.

Create a LAIR. Where there are people, there are conflicts. But not all conflict is bad. When seen as an opportunity for exchange, growth, and success, conflict can be an important step in the development of any relationship.

The key to turning conflict into cooperation is assertive communication. Because it respects the rights of all the concerned parties, assertion is the only behavior that can lead to a win-win solution.

To communicate assertively, remember: LAIR.

L. *Listen*. Assertive listening (see pp. 81–85) requires an active commitment to the worth and integrity of the other party. Think of your eyes, posture, facial expressions, position of your arms and legs, and verbal feedback as opportunities to demonstrate the high regard you have for that person (as high as the regard you have for yourself). In other words, listen unto others as you would have them listen unto you. Turn off the TV, plug in the answering machine, stop trying to find something to do with your hands, and pay attention.

A. *Acknowledge*. Show that you understand and take the message you've received seriously by rephrasing it in your own words: "Let me see if I understand you right: . . . ." Focus as much attention on the intent of your communicant's message as the words and the body language used.

I. *Inquire*. Ask the kind of open-ended questions that provide your communicant with opportunities to suggest possible solutions: "I understand how you feel about . . . . What do you think we can do about . . . ?" And don't rush to fill in your solution if the person doesn't answer right away. Be patient; you'll get your chance. What's important now is to show sincere regard for your communicant's viewpoints and feelings.

R. *Respond*. Make your first responses positive (thank the person for his or her input; mention the points where you agree). In the areas of possible disagreement, state your feelings honestly and directly but delay making any judgments or determining any solutions. When you evaluate another's position, you reduce the conversation to an "I'm right, you're wrong" premise. When you rush to state a solution, you send the message that you're smarter than the other person — so smart that you're able to figure out a solution without really discussing the issue. You've heard what the person has to say, asked a few questions, and pronounced.

More important than determining who's right or what the next course of action should be is creating an atmosphere that allows you and your communicant (read: future partner) to be open and direct with your thoughts and feelings. In other words, you want to establish the foundation of trust and respect on which your negotiations for a win-win solution will be based.

Learning to behave assertively requires time, effort, and patience. Make your first attempts in the areas where your risks are lowest. Your success will give you the confidence and experience you need to take on progressively greater challenges, assert yourself more effectively with clients, customers, colleagues and, yes, even bosses.

22
How to Combat Job Burnout

We burn out at our jobs when we're no longer motivated to work. And it doesn't happen overnight. Rather, it starts in small ways that are almost imperceptible from the frustration, anxiety, and depression that exist from time to time in every job. The difference with burnout is that the frustration, anxiety, and depression occur more frequently and last longer. Our physical resistance to colds and viruses declines, we may sleep the same amount of time but feel less rested, and our ability to concentrate becomes increasingly difficult. Eventually, we give up trying; we no longer care. Our jobs and to some extent our lives have become meaningless.

The key to reversing burnout, motivation, is easier to discuss than it is to achieve. The reason for this is that most people feel they have to be motivated in order to work effectively. Few realize that motivation is also determined by how you feel *after* you've acted. If you can force yourself to work hard and achieve some initial success, you will be on the road toward regaining your lost motivation.

Forget, momentarily, the boss who only notices when you do something wrong, the client who is never satisfied, the in-basket that's always full, the low pay, boring tasks, and lack of recognition. These forces, which have robbed you of your confidence and self-control, will still be there when you've regained your can-do attitude and are ready to meet them on more equal footing.

For now, you need to retake charge of your life. You need to restore some of that personal power that's been siphoned away from you over the last months or years.

Here's how:

Set a goal. A small one is best because it will increase your chances for a crucial early success. In fact, you should set yourself up to succeed. To do this, your goal should be specific, measurable, and completed within a certain amount of time (see pp. 11–12). Achieving your goal will enable you to regain some of the control over your lost life. The confidence and motivation you need to set another small, easy-to-achieve goal will not be far behind.

And be sure to reward yourself (e.g., a pat on the back, a break from work, or a special restaurant for lunch) whenever you achieve a goal.

Control those stress factors. When animals, even the human ones, are threatened, they generally respond in one of two ways: they fight or they flee. As a casualty of burnout, you've lost the motivation to do either. You've become bored, depressed, and lethargic. Meanwhile, your stress level has soared. On the outside, you may appear subdued but, on the inside, stress is wreaking havoc on your body and making you tired and miserable.

To reduce your stress level, identify the causes of your anxiety and take the steps necessary to regain control of your life.

Turn to your friends. You may not want to do this, but friends can be particularly helpful when you're suffering from burnout. Share your feelings and your plans for recovery with the ones you most trust. If they really are your friends, they'll reinforce your sense of self-worth by reminding you of the important qualities you momentarily forgot you possessed.

They may also have some advice from when they were in a similar position. If they don't offer any advice (some people think they're better friends when they just listen), ask them for their suggestions. They'll be flattered, you'll be given an alternative to consider, and the bond of your friendship will be strengthened.

Shift your focus. Many jobs are defined by the people who last held them. When new people are hired, they're trained to complete tasks the same ways as their predecessors. Remind yourself that you weren't hired to copy another person's behavior; you were hired to solve a problem. Identify that problem and see if you can come up with a different way of dealing with it. There may be more flexibility in your job than you think; perhaps you can tailor your tasks to be more in line with your own wants and needs. Few people, for example, are hired just to answer the phone; they're hired to effectively help all the people who call. Why were you hired?

Set your priorities. Make a list of the tasks you perform at work; then rate these tasks as "More Important," "Important," and "Less Important."

Once you've rated your tasks, ask yourself how many of the "Less Important" tasks you can eliminate from your work schedule or delegate to someone more temperamentally suited to complete them.

From your list of "More Important" and "Important" tasks, establish an order of priorities. Which ones you want to work on first, second, third, and so on. Don't feel you have to put all your "More Important" tasks at the top of your list and all you "Important" ones at the bottom. Begin with a "More Important" task, then consider listing one that you enjoy doing. The second task will be your reward for completing the first one.

Take on new responsibilities. If you're bored with your job, perhaps you're no longer challenged by it. Fill the time you've created by eliminating your "Less Important" tasks with ones that aren't in your job description or aren't necessarily the province of any single person or department. Look for responsibilities that will challenge you and you think you will enjoy performing. Consider delaying any request for permission to work on these new tasks until after you've completed them. Then show your results to whomever has the authority to assign you the task.

Keep your job. Many authorities on burnout suggest quitting your job and finding one that is more suitable to what you want in your work, but anyone who has ever had to depend on a paycheck knows the perils of this advice. Even if you could find another job, there's no guarantee that it would be much better than the one you already have.

A more reasonable, realistic, and responsible approach is to take the time to discover what in your present job has caused you to become burned out. If you can correct the problem, you might not need to find another job or, if you do change jobs, you can work to prevent what happened in your present job from reoccurring.

Keep the faith. If you think you're unable to control your life and see yourself as losing more often than you can win, you're only perpetuating your own powerlessness. The major difference between burnout and motivation is Right Attitude. Think powerful, positive thoughts, and you can turn your depression, frustration and failure into optimism, confidence, and success.

23

How to Be More Creative

Visiting a New York City public high school, the great educator Horace Mann walked into a classroom of seniors, picked up a piece of chalk, and drew a small, filled-in circle on the class's blackboard. "What is that?" he asked the students. Over 90 percent of the students said the mark was a dot; the rest said it was a period.

Mann repeated this exercise in a third-grade class. The students had 27 different ideas about what the mark could be. Everything from "my father's bald head to the eye of God."

What happens to us between the third and twelfth grades? Right-side brain damage.

In 1981, Roger Sperry won the Nobel Prize for his theory that the brain is divided into two hemispheres: the left side and the right side. The left side of our brain controls logical, linear, and analytical thinking; the right controls imaginative, creative, impulsive thinking. Although the two sides are distinct, their function is to overlap. When we recall the face of a person, for example, we use the right side of our brain; when we remember the name associated with the face, we use the left side.

Unfortunately, our schools reward left-side brain activities (remembering facts and repeating them on an exam, for example) more than right-side brain experiences (creating ideas and exploring their possibilities). The result is that we all have over-developed, left-sided.

Creative people have found ways to free the right sides of their brains from the controlling influences of the left side. How many times have you been mentally blocked at your desk only to have the solution you needed pop into your mind hours later while showering or walking your dog? Released from the pressure of thinking logically, your mind was now open to receive messages from the spontaneous, impulsive, intuitive, artistic, holistic, right side. To create the most effective solutions to your problems:

Change your attitude. The Right Attitude for thinking creatively is essentially anarchist. It refuses to slip into the lazy habit of upholding the status quo. This includes everything from trying something new for lunch to testing a company's time-honored way of solving a problem. In other words, creative people take risks. Without risk and its frequent companion failure, the kind of success that leads to advancement simply isn't possible.

The Wrong Attitude *vs.*	*The Right Attitude*
This is the way we've always done it.	Let's try it this way. Let's see what happens. What have we got to lose? How much can we gain?
It takes too much time.	We never have time to think through a project but we always have time to correct a mistake.
It costs too much.	How much will we save in the long run? If we lose here, what will we gain elsewhere?
That's not my job.	I'd like the opportunity.
That's not how we do it.	What would happen if we tried to . . . ?
Our clients would never go for this.	What's the worst that could happen?
You may be right, but	You're right and . . . .
It's good enough as it is.	What can we do to make it better?
What's the right way?	What's a better way?
Is it correct?	Does it work? Is this the most effective way?
This is serious.	This could be fun.
What do the experts say?	What do the experts know?

Think with your eyes, not with your head. Cluster! Yes, gentle reader, it's back: the world's most effective brainstorming technique (see pp. 32–35).

Begin with a blank piece of paper. Write in the middle of the paper the name of whatever you want to think about. Circle this focus of your thoughts and relax. Whatever ideas come into your mind (don't try to think of any; let them come naturally), add them to your cluster, draw a circle around each idea, and connect the circle with the circle that led to it.

For example, if I wanted to think about some of the ways clustering can be used, my cluster might look something like this:

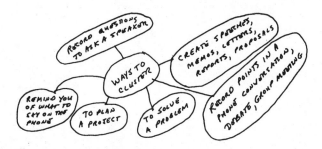

Remember: Creative thinking is all in your mind. Whether you think you can or you think you can't, you're right.

24

How to Take Risks

Eric Fromm tells us that if we could be conscious at the moment of birth we would have two simultaneous impulses: to stay where it's safe and to try something new. These impulses, he says, remain with us for the rest of our lives and form the basis of every decision we make from what we have for breakfast to whether we take an overseas job.

Those who stay put tend to be conservative. The few risks they take are usually made to preserve a status quo, even when that status quo may not be as comfortable as the alternative they're avoiding. Although there are many famous conservatives, the groundbreakers of history were all risk-takers. Not content with the way things were, even when the comfort zones they created for themselves were large and varied, the risk-takers continually sought new opportunities to change themselves and, to the chagrin of the conservatives, others.

If you tend to think of risk as something negative (every risk involves the threat of change and loss) you have to change your attitude as well as your behavior. To have the Right Attitude, consider risk taking as an investment in your future, as an opportunity to discover and grow, and as a challenge that must be met to remain competitive. For you the question may not be "Should I take risks?" but "What risks contain the fewest possibilities for loss?" The pay-off for these risks is not very great but, if you're threatened by change, this is a safe place to begin.

To become more comfortable with the change risk entails, start small: be positive, set goals, say "no" for a change, express how you really feel, question why, submit a proposal, shorten a deadline, take a class in a subject you know little about, make a videotape about the people where you work. In other words, challenge yourself with opportunities to change your behavior. You won't be disappointed, you'll be better prepared to take greater risks later on, and you may be surprised at what you discover.

The more comfortable you can become with change, the more willing and able you'll be to take risks. And the more likely you'll be to benefit from them. Not all your risks will be successful, but you can increase your chances of success and minimize the possibilities of failure.

Here's how:

Clarify your goals. Focus specifically on what you want. The more specific and less general you can be the better the position you'll be in to determine what risks to take and what risks to avoid.

Determine a strategy. All risks entail the possibility of loss, but some losses are greater than others. What's the greatest loss you can absorb without permanently damaging your ability to reach your goal? Is any risk worth suffering this loss? What losses are worth suffering? Can these losses be minimized by creating a series of incremental risks that culminate in your goal? If so, any losses on your ladder to success can be seen as temporary setbacks and opportunities for learning what not to repeat.

Increase your chances of success. You can improve your odds for success and reduce your chances for a loss by gathering additional information. Perhaps there are some books or articles you can read or people you can interview without impinging too severely on your time (a delay might give someone else the advantage) or your resources (not every expenditure of money or energy can be recovered by a better decision).

To get the feedback you need from your colleagues and subordinates, ask for opinions and feelings rather than conclusions and solutions, explain why alternative viewpoints will help you make a better decision, and ask if you're doing something to discourage others from communicating openly and honestly.

Decide. In many ways, deciding is tougher than acting. But not to decide is to stagnate, which is a form of action but not the kind you want. To help yourself reach an effective and timely decision, consider the risk you're contemplating from another viewpoint. Ask your friends for their opinions if you have difficulty creating a new perspective on your own.

Act. Once you've made your decision, go for it. To wonder if you've done the right thing is only natural (like "buyer's remorse") so don't let it stop you. Yes, you're putting yourself in some kind of jeopardy, but it shouldn't last long and you won't be better off than you are now unless you move beyond the comfort zone that's already started to strangle you. Your comfort zone is one of the reasons (though you may not be consciously aware of it) why you've decided to risk change.

Evaluate. Not all your risks or every part of each risk will be successful, but you can turn your worst failure into the kind of positive learning experience that will reduce the risk in your next attempt at change. Sometimes, when you just miss reaching your goal, failure can be a motivating force. Now you know you can do it; it's just a matter of repeating what worked and avoiding what didn't.

Risk again. Whatever you gain through risk will eventually degenerate into another comfort zone. Before your new comfort zone forces you to change, imagine new systems, processes, and designs. In other words, dream! Learn to live everyday with the idea of change. Better yet, learn to love it.

25

How to Handle Sexual Harassment

You are your first line of defense against sexual harassment. Act like the professional you know yourself to be, focus on the job you were hired to do, and leave sexual game-playing for the bored who need to fill a vacuum in their lives.

General guideline: ignore gender unless absolutely necessary. Make a point of using parallel language (e.g., "man and woman" and "husband and wife" instead of "man and wife"), favoring words that includes both sexes (e.g., "salesperson" or "sales representative" instead of "salesman"), and avoid dividing your profession by gender (e.g., "lawyers" and "lady lawyers"). Also always be sure to give men and women equal treatment (e.g., "John Doe and Mary Brown" instead of "John Doe and Mary"). These are small things, but each one sends an important signal.

Unfortunately, there are sexually biased men and women wherever you go. Ignore them. Don't laugh at their jokes, respond to their innuendos, or even participate in a conversation that's not related to business. Because many of these people aren't aware of their biases, they'll make you look like the aggressor if you confront them (e.g., "What's the matter? Can't you take a joke?").

For the less than innocent, act quickly and decisively. Challenge the first use of any endearing terms (e.g., "You're such a sweetie!") by telling your offender that you don't find these terms complimentary. Using a term that implies a relationship that extends beyond the boundaries of business is usually a test. If you respond positively or not at all, consider yourself failed.

133

The next overture, if there is one, will not be so subtle; so you prepare by being more businesslike than ever in the company of this person. If you're asked to "meet for coffee" or invited "to get together some time after work," change the subject to something related to your job, hope that he or she takes your hint. You don't want to hurt anyone's feelings if you don't have to. Someone who's been rejected may want to get even. Your goal is to say "no" without losing his or her professional respect. And here's one way to do that: State politely but firmly that you don't "see," "meet," or "go out with" anyone you work with.

And don't get trapped into a dialogue explaining why. You just don't do it.

This kind of unwarranted and unsolicited behavior becomes harassment the very first time it makes you feel uncomfortable and interferes with your ability to do your job.

Here's what to do:

Confront. Tell the person you're not interested and to stop bothering you or, if he or she continues, you'll be forced to take more severe measures.

Inform. Tell a senior person of the same sex as the offender what's been going on and ask for his or her suggestion on what to do.

Record. Start keeping a log of what the offender has said and done. Note place, date, time, circumstances, and how you responded.

Write. Confirm what's been taking place in a letter and make an appointment with your company's Equal Employment Opportunity officer to have the letter formally placed in your personnel file.

Work. Keep doing your job, create as much distance as you can between you and the offender, and don't be afraid. Remember: You can handle the situation, you *don't* have to accept anything that offends you, and there *are* people at every level in every organization who *will* help you.

26

How to Have a Family and a Career

If you want to work for any reason other than need (i.e., you could use the extra money, you don't want to interrupt your career, you enjoy a challenge, staying home is boring) think twice about working before your children are old enough to be left at home without your supervision. Your children need you and the consistent, supportive structure your presence at home provides to help them through the crucial formative years of their lives. To *choose* to give them anything less is irresponsible.

Your children also need your attention and love — lots of it. And they don't understand the concept of "quality time." You may set aside a certain Saturday morning to give your children your undivided attention but, when that time comes, your children may prefer to watch television or play with their friends. See the idea of quality time for what it is: a rationalization to allow parents to do what they want or need to do and not feel guilty.

If you must work, here are your options:

A *full-time job*. Or rather a second full-time job to compete with the full-time job of raising your kids. To get the most for your family out of a full-time job, participate in a program that includes "flextime" (i.e., variable hours for starting and leaving work) or "compressed time" (i.e., working 10 to 12 hours a day). The former allows you to arrange your work schedule around your children's schedules; the latter gives you more time at home.

A part-time job. This is a good solution in terms of time, but part-time employment is low-paying and often without benefits. Adding injury to injury, part-time workers are often assigned the least challenging tasks or work no one else wants to do, are often supervised by people they should be supervising, are by-passed for promotions, are frequently seen and treated as "temporary help," and are given few opportunities to contribute to their careers.

A recent innovation in part-time work is job sharing. In this scheme, two people share the same job. One may work two days one week and three the next or work alternate weeks. How job sharers divide their time is up to them and their employers. Although complicated to implement, job sharing can benefit employers if each of the job sharers not only share the same basic skills but also has individual strengths to contribute to the success of the company.

Self-employment. A good alternative if you have a marketable skill (teachers can tutor, secretaries can type, writers can write, executives can consult, and anyone can babysit or sell over the phone) is to work for yourself, but no solution is perfect. You can't, for example, simultaneously tutor a student and change a diaper. And people who work out of their homes often feel isolated and understimulated.

Arranging Child Care at Home

If you have to work, your biggest challenge is child care, which is an historically low priority of business, government, and industry. Look to the members of your extended family. Especially grandparents who love you and your children and are free, able, and willing to help you raise them.

"Raise" is the key word here. You want a person who is comfortable with your children and with whom they feel comfortable. The person must also be capable of maintaining a consistent, daily routine and, over a long period of time, the continuity necessary for your children's sense of security. You want a person who contributes positively to your children's well-being and who has your family's interests at heart. Few people come closer to filling this bill than grandparents.

If grandparents are unavailable or unwilling to help, you need what is known in the babysitting industry as a child-care provider. It's no secret and it's no joke that most people care more about who drives their cars than who watches their kids.

So solicit the recommendations of friends and relatives, ask your would-be babysitters for references, and check them out. The more serious and competent an image you can present to any prospective provider, the more serious the one you hire will be about what they do for you.

And don't hire anyone without at least one substantial interview. Ask questions of your prospective child-care provider that begin with statements such as "What would you do if . . . ?" You don't want to hire someone who doesn't share your values or wouldn't do something very close to what you would do in the same situation.

Your children should also participate in the interview. Watch how they get along with your prospective provider. Do they go to the person or stay near you? Does the provider make an attempt to make your children feel comfortable or does the provider keep talking to you as if your children aren't there? Find an excuse to leave the room for a few minutes and, when you return, notice how your children and their would-be babysitter get along.

If the provider will be watching your children in your home, explain what you want the children to do and not do. Your children, if they're old enough, should be present so it's clear to them that you are giving the provider the authority to act in your place.

Arranging Child Care at a Center

If you decide to send your children to a day-care or after-school center, make an appointment to visit the center a few days later, drop by unexpected. While visiting the center, talk to the children about their likes and dislikes, ask the head of the center for the names of several parents you can contact, discuss the daily activities your children will regularly participate in, inquire about the methods of instruction and discipline, and bring your children to the center to see how they respond.

If you decide to send your children to a day-care or after-school center, establish a relationship with the providers; consider bringing them an occasional gift. When you pick up your children, talk to the providers about the events in their lives. Something might be happening at the center that will explain a child's recent behavior at home.

Whether your children stay at home or go to a center, they should know why you work and what that means in terms they can understand. If your children are old enough to play sports, for example, you can explain your job as similar to playing on a team. Bring your children to the place where you work, let them see the pictures of themselves on your desk and, if you think it appropriate, introduce your children to some of your colleagues. That way they will know who you are talking about when you talk about your job. They'll know the team players.

If you believe your children are mature enough to stay at home without immediate supervision:

Know each of your children's daily schedule and have them telephone you every day as soon as they get home from school. Plan your daily work schedule with their call in mind so you can take some time to chat with your children about their day.

List by the home phone: your telephone number at work, the numbers of a nearby relative and several friends, and your family address (in an emergency, children can forget things like this). Make sure your children know all about 911. If you allow your children to answer the phone, they should be taught never to say "No one's home."

If you allow your children to answer the door when no adult is present, make sure they know who's on the other side before opening it. Perhaps a friend or relative could look in on your children each afternoon before you get home from work.

Teach your children to keep all the doors and windows locked until you get home. If one of your children thinks someone might be following him or her home from school, your child should know to to go a neighbor's house or a store and ask for help. If a stranger approaches one of your children on the street, your child should be rehearsed in an effective response: "My mom's waiting for me at the corner." Consider some role-playing sessions just to make sure your children can't be easily fooled.

If one of your children is sick or injured, you may have to leave work. Even with a boss who is sympathetic, make sure your absence will not delay any important projects. Tell your boss why you have to leave, what work you're taking with you, and when you will have it completed.

Getting Help Around the House

See your home and your job as parts of your total day. When creating your to do list (see pp. 16–18), include every waking hour in your schedule. You can run errands during your lunch break, for example, bring office work home, and delegate household responsibilities. Discuss with your children, if they're old enough, and your spouse or significant other what chores need to be done. Decide with your family who will be responsible for what chores and be sure your children understand that they're not being forced to do these tasks because you work. Doing chores is the responsibility of every family member.

Some children and even some adults may have to be taught how to complete certain tasks. Be patient with your instructions and praise even the smallest accomplishments. Accept the fact that no job will be done as well as you can do it. What's important is that the job be done as well as your child or partner can do it.

Some family counselors suggest that your children's household chores be tied to their allowances; others say the chores and allowances should be kept separate. All therapists agree, however, that the family members should work together as a team to complete some tasks individually (e.g., making their own beds, keeping their own rooms clean) and some together (e.g., washing the windows, cleaning the basement). No child should be so overwhelmed with work that their studies or recreational time become interrupted.

As a team member, a parent can complete a child's tasks in the days preceding an exam or during the time that a child must devote to working on an important assignment. At times such as these or in families where school and careers don't leave much time for household chores, an easy and practical solution may be to hire outside help.

Creating Time

The secret to creating time is to schedule specific hours into your daily plan. Discuss with your family members what they'd like to do together and separately. Friday might, for example, could be reserved for the family to go to a movie, Saturday morning for shooting hoops with your eldest child, a certain hour of every evening. The best time is right after the kids are in bed (for you and your mate). Take the phone off the hook, leave the grease on the stove a little longer, forget about the next day's meeting, and relax. If you don't create time for the two of you, it won't happen by itself.

Also, make time for yourself: an occasional longer lunch break, an evening with friends, a trip to the gym. You need it and you deserve it.

Combating Guilt

The fact that you're missing important events in your child's life, that you're not participating in your child's activities to the degree that you should, that you can't work and give your family the time it deserves, that no day-care center is adequate, that every school has its deficiencies, that your spouse/partner never sees you anymore, that your babysitter spends more time with your child than you do, and that your performance at work isn't what it should be are only a few of the reasons to feel guilty about working, even when you have to work.

Resist the temptation to compensate for your guilt with extra gifts for your children or allowing your children to go undisciplined or your significant other to be irresponsible. And don't blame yourself for everything that didn't go exactly the way you planned it. Your family will see what motivates your behavior and could be tempted to use your guilt to take advantage of you.

If you have to work to support your family, staying at home isn't an option and you have no reason to feel guilty. If staying at home is an option and you've weighed your decision to work against your family's needs to have you in the house, you already know that what's in your best interests is also in the best interests of your family. If you're unhappy, they'll be unhappy. Again, you have no reason to feel guilty. If friends and relatives think you're a bad parent because you work, nothing you do will change their minds. So don't try and don't allow them to change your mind. However guilty you may feel because of others' viewpoints is nothing compared to how you will feel when you act according to their value systems.

Instead of trying to assuage your guilt by complaining about your job, focus on making your family feel good about the work you do. Start by letting them see how working makes you happy. Show your family the place where you work. When they see the photographs of themselves, the gifts they've given you, and the pinned-up drawings your children made for you, they'll know that even though you're at work you're always thinking of them.

And when you come home from work, don't just tell them how much you miss them, show them.

Part 5

Leading
Others

A leader is best when people barely know he
exists. They will say "We did this ourselves."
LAO TSE

27

How to Supervise

Two management styles dominate business and industry: the dictator and the benevolent dictator.

The dictator style, which rose out of the industrial revolution, reached its apex some time before the rise of unions. Its use isn't as widespread as it was four decades ago, but it is still relied on to resolve many problems.

The premise for the dictator philosophy is that people don't like to work and, left to their own devices, will do as little of it as possible, that the most effective motivator is a combination of reward and punishment, that security is more important than challenge and opportunity, and that the boss appointed by the company is right because he or she is the boss appointed by the company. In this system, the boss tells the workers what to do and the workers do what they are told. The workers are task-oriented, externally motivated, have no authority, and have minimal responsibility. In short, they are treated as children.

The benevolent dictator style, which rose in popularity between the two World Wars, is management's response to the power and influence of unions. Its premise is that people can be motivated more effectively by rewards than threats and punishment, that people will seek greater challenges and take on more responsibility if their work satisfies a personal as well as a company need, and that people who are committed don't have to be monitored as closely as those who work because they have to, thus freeing managers and supervisors to focus on other tasks.

In this system, the boss's relationship with the workers is more casual and less authoritative. The workers feel they can make suggestions; sometimes they are even asked for advice. This opportunity to participate in decisions gives the workers a sense of control over their lives. This sense of control, in turn, strengthens their commitment to the company's goals. Unfortunately for the workers, their sense of control is more illusion than fact. While they may have greater access to their bosses, the workers still have no decision-making authority. Treated like adolescents whose responsibilities increase as they get older but whose decision-making authority does not enjoy a corresponding rise, these workers often behave like adolescents: mature some days and not so mature on other days.

Many managers prefer the benevolent dictator style because it gives their authority a human face without taking away any of their power. Required to be police officers only part of the time, they can focus more on what they were hired to do: figure out ways to make their workers more productive.

Most managers today started out as benevolent dictators. They wanted to please the company and have a good relationship with their workers. They soon discovered, however, that the very qualities that enabled them to become managers (dedication, hard work, self-sacrifice) weren't universally practiced by the people they were hired to manage. Having been under the thumb of authority figures since the day they were born (parents, teachers, clergy, officers, and other managers) many of the workers had learned to get by with as little work as possible in order to achieve the grades, money, or time they needed to do what they really wanted to do. As a result, would-be benevolent managers found themselves relying more and more on dictator tactics. If they didn't resort to these tactics, they feared production would suffer and they'd lose their jobs.

The dictator style has proven to work best where the workers' focus is primarily on tasks: getting x amount of work done in y amount of time. In this situation, the dictator has all of the power and nothing to lose but his or her job. The benevolent dictator is more effective when the manager has less power and is forced to rely on more subtle methods to influence the workers. In these situations, the manager's effectiveness depends on the relationship with the workers and the particular kinds of tasks that have to be accomplished.

To help their managers succeed as benevolent dictators, many companies train their managers in techniques on how to handle situations rather than relate to people (e.g., "What to do if . . . "). Managers trained in situation-response skills might appear as benevolent when addressing a group of workers but resort to dictator techniques when talking in private to an individual worker.

The fashion in management structure today, however, is team-building (see pp. 181–195). In this scheme, decision-making power that was once the province of managers is now shared with teams of workers. Managers, now called "leaders," "coordinators," or "facilitators," are expected to be "team players" as well. Resistance for the team-building concept has come from two obvious sources: the managers (who don't want to give up their power) and the workers (who don't want to be responsible for the decisions they're now being asked to make).

Regardless of the management structure in your organization and of what you may be called, there are certain characteristics that the most successful managers, supervisors, leaders, coaches, directors, chairs, heads, coordinators, and facilitators share:

They're not afraid of success. The best leaders don't worry that their achievements might inspire others to be jealous, envious, or begrudging. Nor do they feel guilty because they're successful and others aren't.

They're capable of taking complex ideas and breaking them down into simple objectives that can be handled one at a time. They don't let much come in the way of their reaching those objectives. In other words, the best leaders focus and they persevere.

They're willing to take risks. The best leaders share their glory when they succeed and take their share of the responsibility when they do not.

They're charismatic. The best leaders don't need the affection, approval, or acceptance of others. They can articulate their thoughts, are comfortable with the praise they receive, and give the appearance of being in control even when they're not. The best leaders don't hesitate to act once a decision has been made, they don't lose their sense of humor, and they never fail to inspire others.

Followers need the energy of leaders to cheer them up, calm them down, or make them feel positive about themselves in some other way. Leaders generate their own energy and use it to charge others.

They are good examples. By constantly setting and working to attain high standards, the best leaders encourage others to excel. They also support rather than compete with the workers who make similar efforts to learn and grow.

They let those in their charge know what's expected of them. The best leaders know that no structure is worse than too much structure, and the best structure is appropriate, clearly stated, challenging, and supportive. Knowing what's expected of them enables workers to focus more efficiently on specific tasks and take better control of their time. This, in turn, gives them a greater sense of freedom and a willingness to participate in areas beyond their assigned tasks.

They're considerate of others. The best leaders show concern for their workers well-being without giving the impression they're evaluating or judging them. Workers feel they can communicate with these leaders without the threat of anyone becoming defensive.

They don't put on airs. The best leaders don't give the impression they're superior to anyone because of the positions they hold. They're followed because they're liked and admired for who they are. Leading by personal rather than positional power, the best leaders make people feel equal even when these same people know they are not.

They don't need to win every argument, be right on every issue, and come out on top in every confrontation. Rather, the best leaders are open to the views of others, analyze perspectives rather than choose sides, prefer working together to telling others what to do, and are more interested in experiment than control.

They appreciate the process of getting to the top more than the satisfaction of having reached it. Never resting on their laurels for long, the best leaders seek new challenges without forgetting where they started from and who helped them along the way.

Ironically, not every effective leader has all of these characteristics, and having all of these traits doesn't guarantee anyone will be a successful leader. Many people possess these qualities. What separates these masses from the leaders is that the leaders have discovered how to make these qualities work for them. They don't waste their time wondering if they have what it takes to be good leaders, they focus on what they can do to help themselves and others reach their goals.

To act as a leader:

Have the right attitude. Having a positive attitude is the single, most powerful weapon in any leader's arsenal. Whether you're charismatic or not, you want to project a winning, optimistic image, and you won't present that image if you allow a negative attitude to undermine you.

Don't rule by role. As a manager, you've been granted a certain amount of power but, as a leader, you don't need it. You want to be respected for whom you are, not what you are. Avoid reminding your workers who's in charge; rely instead on your knowledge, experience, and ability to establish rapport with people. The more effective you are at using these skills, the more respect you'll earn and the less you'll have to rely on the authority that has been given you.

Create a vision. Leaders know where they're going because they have goals. They create their own futures; they don't let others do it for them — not much of it anyway, or at least not for long. Ironically, the best leaders' visions are rarely self-serving. Employees follow and remain loyal to leaders who demonstrate that their visions will make a difference in the lives of all concerned.

Act on your vision. Discuss your vision with others not once, but many times. Demonstrate how serious you are about reaching your goals by behaving in ways that are consistent with the vision you describe. Develop strategies for the long- and short-term, start working on what needs to be done soonest, become a role model and mentor for others, plan for the growth and development of those in your charge, and reward every attempt at change, even the failed ones.

Free yourself to lead. You can't keep abreast of trends, plan for the future, and make the kinds of decisions necessary to establish yourself as a leader if you're bogged down in the day-to-day running of a department. Delegate (see pp. 157–161)! If your employees can't make a decision without your approval, your job as their leader is to increase their responsibilities in the decision-making process. If they don't have the behavioral or technical skills to assume an increased share of that responsibility, your job is to arrange for them to develop these skills. If they're given the skills but don't have the confidence to take the necessary risks, your job as their leader is to reward them for the risks they do take, even when they fail, and encourage them to continue seeking greater responsibilities.

Take risks. Playing it safe is not a leadership quality, but what do you do if one of your carefully calculated risks fails? Accept the responsibility, suffer the consequences, learn from your mistakes, and go on. Your company's loss wasn't just a cost; it was a serious investment in your education.

When someone in your charge takes a risk and fails, reward the person for having the courage to try something new and stress the lesson that failures are only failures when we fail to learn from them.

Facilitate change. Leaders are rarely satisfied with any status quo, but many people are rarely satisfied with anything else. They see change as a threat. To ease the fear of change in others, reward those who try something new (even when they don't try hard enough to succeed), make change desirable by demonstrating the limitations of the present way of doing things (a change in process can be used to make the old ways ineffective), focus on the benefits of change as soon as any occurs (if you wait for everyone to back your enthusiasm for change, it will never happen).

Because there is no single, sure-fire way to be an effective leader, you have to develop your own style and philosophy. Experiment! Whatever works is your style; the reason why is your philosophy.

28

How to Deal with Difficult People

Guess what? All the people in the world can be divided into four personality groups. Although each of us possess characteristics common to all four groups, one trait will point to a specific group. If you can identify the dominant characteristic in any person you have to deal with (difficult or not), all you have to do is consult this chapter for clues as to how to influence him or her.

The four personality categories have different names depending on whom you read (they were discovered by Hippocrates), but the traits and their divisions are all the same. For our purposes we'll label these categories: the Director, the Relator, the Thinker, and the Operator.

Directors

Directors are your self-contained, focused types who like to take charge of people and projects. Businesslike, functional, and pragmatic, they get things done ahead of time. Most managers have Director personalities because Directors achieve quickly and are rewarded sooner than most other types. Interested in results, they set and meet their goals, are more concerned with what something does than how it works, place more importance on success than relationships, thrive on competition, and measure their worth by what they've accomplished.

To motivate Directors, you want to support their goals (they all have goals) and reward them for the work they've done (they can get more tasks completed in a day than many others can do in a week). In spite of their independence and single-minded ability to focus, Directors tend to follow strong leaders. Lee Iacocca embodies the best in a Director.

Directors work better with goals than with people, learn by doing, are irritated by inefficiency and indecision, and would rather be respected than liked. Directors are likely to interrupt you in the middle of a task and tell you, "Here, let me do it." The Director's way is not only the right way, it's the only way.

For this reason, you must always allow your Directors to feel as if they're in charge even if you're the supervisor. Because Directors are the only ones who know how to complete any task, you must never tell them what to do. Give them options instead and let them decide. The Directors' greatest fear is losing control; this is why they're not happy until they're in a position to tell everybody else what to do while complaining that no one can do anything as well as they can.

Relators

Unlike Directors, who focus on what, Relators focus on who. They're "people persons." Appearing more casual than the businesslike Directors, Relators are personal, relaxed, and friendly. More easy-going than decisive, more interested in relationships than results, motivated more by attention than accomplishment, and believing that relationships offer more security than success, Relators want to know how their behavior affects their personal circumstances. Will they be more or less liked?

To motivate Relators, support their feelings, show a personal interest in their private lives, and listen actively. The effect of your eyes glazing over during a conversation with a Relator can be devastating because you show you don't care enough to pay attention. Relators want to have influence without being in charge, are irritated by insecurity, and learn through observing and sharing rather than doing.

Since the Relators' greatest fear is rejection, workers always point to Relators as their favorite managers. Relator managers tend to be democratic, flexible, and interested more in the interests of the group than the completion of tasks. In other words, they're team players as well as team leaders. They share their glory and measure their worth by how well they get along with others.

Thinkers

Thinkers want to know why. This is their greatest strength as well as their biggest weakness. Enthusiastic compilers of information, they rarely get anything done on time.

Thinkers dress more conservatively than Relators but, unlike Directors, aren't necessarily businesslike. Structured, organized, and functional, they're also slow, systematic, and overly concerned with details. Few things please them as much as burying themselves in a library or laboratory for hours. The more prepared they are for any endeavor, the more insecure they feel because in learning so much about any subject they've discovered how much they don't know and it frightens them.

To motivate your Thinkers, support their thoughts, their ability to analyze, and their thorough approach to every project. However, you also have to keep a gun at their heads to complete anything they work on because Thinkers also tend to be perfectionists. Setting impossibly high standards for themselves and fearing criticism more than anything else, they suffer terminally from a disease known as "paralysis by analysis."

They hate surprises, are threatened by unpredictability, and are unmoved by apology. Tell a Thinker you're sorry and you're likely to hear "Sorry doesn't make it better." You can tell a Relator you're sorry more times than you can count and you will almost always be forgiven, but you have to *show* Thinkers how truly sorry you are.

Because Thinkers measure their worth by how precise, deliberate, correct, and thorough they are, you appeal to them through logic rather than emotion. Thinkers aren't called "Thinkers" and Relators aren't called "Relators" for nothing.

Operators

Operators don't usually play the role of leader but no leader can do without his or her Operators. Loyal, dependable, and consistent to the point of boredom, Operators find joy in repetition. The more they do something, the better they like it, and the more secure they feel.

Operators, with their love of stamps, rubber bands, staples, and cubbyholes, make great postal workers. Operators want to be accountable, value compliance, follow policy, focus on procedures, work well within a structure, want to know the limits of their responsibilities, learn by doing the same thing over and over, have an aptitude for documentation, prefer to monitor rather than direct and, probably above all else, are afraid of losing their jobs.

To motivate an operator, support their plans. And don't worry: Operators are so cautious they never take more than the most minimal of risks. These are the ones you name "Employee of the Month" and set aside a parking space for.

Because Directors focus, Thinkers analyze, and Operators busy themselves with tasks, they are not always as good at listening as Relators. Here are some suggestions for getting through to them:

When the Directors' minds wander. These are the listeners who are physically present but mentally distant. They can be identified by the glaze that comes over their eyes when someone else speaks. To keep the mind-wanderer's attention, lean forward, maintain eyecontact, and stop talking. When your mindwanderer realizes you've stopped talking, ask something of interest to him or her.

When the Thinkers become overly critical. These are the critics who listen but find something wrong with so many different things you're saying that they lose sight of the big picture. So, establish rapport with small talk, be patient, and then present the big picture before you discuss the individual parts.

When the Relators are too compliant. Relators often say they agree (even when they don't) because they don't want to be criticized. To get Relators to be more honest, express your fears and then ask them to comment on what you said. Then reward them by agreeing (at least initially) with whatever they say.

As each of these examples illustrates, the way to influence another person's behavior is to change your own behavior. This is especially true for handling difficult people.

Here are some other things to keep in mind when you're having trouble getting through to people:

Focus on the issue. Bringing personal traits into your discussion only shifts attention away from solving the problem and makes any resolution more difficult. To encourage your correspondent to contribute, ask him how the problem should be solved. People who have a say in reaching a solution are usually more committed to making that solution a success.

Don't respond in kind. The eye-for-an-eye, tooth-for-a-tooth mentality only leaves everyone blind and toothless. When the victim is damaged as much as the offender and the victim reciprocates in equal measure, the resulting negative spiral is ineffective at best and, at worst, danger-ous.

Recognize your limits. Every story has two sides. As accurate as your perspective may be, empathize with your correspondent and see the issue from her perspective. Assume that everything your correspondent says is true.

Be patient. Responding immediately and emotionally to a difficult person only undermines your relationship. Especially if you're angry. Try to free your mind from any prejudices or emotional impulses and reply in a calm, reasonable manner.

Think of difficult behavior as a problem that you and your correspondent have to solve. Work on it objectively as you would any other problem.

Don't lose sight of the big picture. Sometimes we get so wrapped up in a particular issue or behavior, we lose our perspective. The problem seems much larger than it really is.

Don't blame anyone. Blaming only reduces your problem to a "right/wrong," "good/bad," "win/lose" issue. Words such as "always" and "never" start to enter the conversation and what was once a problem has now escalated into a conflict as well.

Be positive. People respond better to praise than criticism and are willing to work more closely with those who appreciate them. Try to catch the difficult people in your life doing something right. Then be sincere and specific in your praise. If this is a new behavior for you, your difficult person may at first be skeptical. Tracking positives is probably the easiest, most risk-free way to improve your relationship with anyone, even the difficult.

29

How to Manage Conflict

Where there are people, there is conflict. But that doesn't mean that there necessarily will be many instances of conflict or that conflict is bad. The Chinese symbol for conflict is a combination of two other symbols: danger and opportunity. Conflict increases the risk for damage but, if handled properly, can also be an effective way to give and receive feedback, discover new solutions to old problems, and increase the chances for success. Effective managers prepare for conflict, use it to everyone's advantage when it occurs, and monitor whatever agreement is reached to make sure it is carried out.

Preparing for Conflict

The best way to prepare for conflict is to remember that resolving it is not about who's right and who's wrong. Resolving conflict is about recognizing and appreciating the differences between people.

The special qualities that make up you are your gifts to whatever you choose to participate in. In dealing with conflict, you want to be receptive and appreciative of others' gifts. To do this, you must remember to preserve at all times the human dignity of everyone involved in a confrontation. Listen carefully to the conflicting views as if each was your own. Feel each speaker's emotional state and remind yourself not to discount someone's viewpoint just because it is different. Finally, accept the fact that you're not going to succeed very often at changing someone's behavior, especially in the middle of a confrontation. There's too much at stake. Focus instead on preparing for what you can say and do when a conflict arises.

If you can anticipate conflict, you also provide yourself with some time to gather information (e.g., What's the history of conflict in this company? With these individuals?) and develop a strategy to prevent the confrontation from escalating.

The most common cause of conflict in any organization is change or the threat of it. Anytime you know that change is on the horizon, you can anticipate a confrontation. Next determine what kind of conflict is likely, who it will involve, and what the opposing views will be.

The fastest and easiest way (though not always the most reliable) to diagnose a conflict is to ask the opinions of those who will be affected by the change. But beware: This method is sometimes unreliable because subordinates are not always candid about their views when talking to someone higher up in the company's power structure. The survivors of countless Flower Revolutions, they've learned that one of the most effective ways to advance a career is to keep their big mouths shut.

You can encourage your subordinates to be more open, honest, and forthcoming with their opinions by expressing your own fears and anxieties. Explain that you need their honest feedback for the benefit of everybody, and don't discourage with a frown or punish with a word anyone whose views differ from your own. In other words, do all you can to help them disagree with you.

From your subordinate's views you should have some clues as to where disagreement is likely to occur. Check back with your workers to see which ones might not have all the information available to them, which ones have misinterpreted the information they do have, and which ones seem to be pursuing their own agendas regardless of what their company has in mind. Then see what you can do to resolve the issue and prevent the conflict from occurring.

Using the Conflict

If disagreement does surface, review your history of conflict in the company and with the individuals involved. What you're witnessing may be the result of long-standing feuds between individuals or even departments. From your history, your observations, and what you've learned from talking with your subordinates, colleagues, and supervisors, see if you can detect a pattern in the conflict. Certainly there should be some consistency in the ways each individual behaves. Identify the predominant personality of each person (e.g., Director, Relator, Thinker, Operator) and refer to the chapter in this book on dealing with difficult people (see pp. 148–152) to determine an approach for resolving the situation.

The first response of most people in a conflict is to try to convince the opposition to accept his or her point of view. This approach almost always fails because the opposition is too busy selling their own ideas. But it's worth trying because, if one party or the other is open to an alternative view, the conflict can be resolved relatively quickly.

Alternative approaches include downplaying the conflict (e.g., "Let sleeping dogs lie"), using an external criteria to resolve the issue (e.g., "Let's draw straws"), bargaining (e.g., "You've got to give a little to get a little"), and deciding not to get involved (e.g., "It'll all blow over"). But these are stop-gap measures at best. They either fail to resolve the conflict or reduce the issue to a win-lose situation.

The most effective approach is to use the conflict to reach a consensus among the competing parties. Work toward developing a synthesis of all the viewpoints and an agreement that everyone involved can live with. No one should get all he wants but no one should be left empty-handed either. Resist putting any matter to a vote. Votes are also a win-lose situation.

To manage by consensus, don't use your position of authority to lend weight to your viewpoint. Stress that your voice should be considered as no more than an equal say, provide a view of the big picture so the conflict and any possible solutions can be seen in their proper context, don't give in to the pressure generated by the more emotional members of your group. Instead invite all to share their opinions, look for areas of agreement that a consensus might be built on, and take all suggestions under consideration seriously.

Important: How you conduct yourself is crucial not only to the outcome of your first conflict but all future conflicts as well. So look relaxed even if you're not (this will give the impression that you're experienced and confident), listen carefully and accept everything that is said as serious (even with what you don't agree), and make every issue a problem for the group to solve (use your authority to direct energy not to enforce viewpoints).

And remember at all times: People have a right to disagree, nobody needs to be reminded of the ways they've behaved badly in the past, and most people will be willing to accept a solution if there is something in it for them.

Monitoring the Agreement

As the members of your work group approach a consensus, begin forging on paper what the ultimate agreement will be. When it is finally reached, type and distribute the agreed-to statements to all the parties in the conflict. Then decide, preferably with your subordinates, how the results will be monitored, by whom, and for how long. In defining these plans for action, consider as many "What if . . ." scenarios as you and your subordinates can possibly brainstorm and how you will respond to each one should it occur.

A Final Note on Conflict Resolution

Perhaps the hardest part of resolving any conflict is defining the problem. Don't be distracted by the symptoms. Alcoholism, for example, is a symptom of a larger problem. Even if you can stop someone from drinking, the cause of the drinking will soon manifest itself in some other area of the person's life.

Placing the issues of the conflict in a cluster (see pp. 32–35) where all the members of the group can see it at once will help your subordinates visualize the problem. Looking at the conflict from the viewpoint of resolution will create a more objective perspective and enable your workers to decide what they had to do to reach the end point from which they're viewing the problem. Finally, encourage your subordinates to work toward the best solution. Sometimes the safest solution is not the most effective.

30

How to Delegate

Delegating responsibility and authority is one of the most effective ways of controlling your future because it frees you to plan and prepare in the present. Delegating, in many ways, is like coaching. The best coaches don't run with the ball (the players do that), and they don't implement techniques (that's what assistants are for). The best coaches focus on strategy.

Like the best coaches, the best managers know that the higher they climb on any corporate ladder, the less time they want to spend on completing tasks that can be done just as well or almost as well or even better by subordinates.

And like the best coaches who groom their assistants to one day become head coaches, the best managers empower those in their charge to grow and develop. They know that effective delegation challenges workers, keeps them from stagnating, demonstrates confidence and trust in them, retains their loyalty and commitment, and expands their horizons. The best delegators, therefore, don't just dump the tasks they don't want to do on their subordinates; the best delegators offer opportunities for their subordinates to learn and advance. In fact, the goal of the very best delegators is to make the task part of their job descriptions obsolete.

Free from details, the best delegators focus on becoming experts on what they were hired to do: manage, supervise, lead, coordinate, mentor, and facilitate. No longer trapped by tasks, the best managers expand their job definitions, increase their contributions, and create more time for themselves and their families. That's the theory, anyway.

The truth is that most managers don't trust their workers to complete many tasks as well as they can. And though these managers may delegate some authority, they know they're still the ones who have to answer for any mistakes that are made. For many managers, then, delegation simply isn't worth the risk of failure and, if they've delegated in the past and got burned, they aren't often willing to get burned again.

Managers who share this viewpoint either fail to understand the meaning of delegation or fail to delegate successfully. The point of delegating is not who can do the better job but rather who has the energy to complete the more important projects. And as for those managers who delegated and got burned, to whom did you delegate? Perhaps your subordinates didn't understand what you wanted them to do; perhaps they lacked the skills or temperament to complete the tasks you assigned; perhaps they felt you were trying to push your work off on them; perhaps they didn't fully appreciate the opportunity you were offering; perhaps they didn't understand what you expected of them; perhaps you delegated responsibility without a corresponding increase in authority; perhaps your workers didn't see anything that would benefit them in your assignments; perhaps there has been a history in your company of managers taking all the glory for work that was mostly done by subordinates.

The first step toward becoming a successful delegator is knowing what to delegate:

Routine tasks. These are the jobs you know so well you can do them in your sleep. Train others to complete these tasks— even the ones you enjoy.

Specialty tasks. Perhaps you have someone who's good with details, another who is imaginative and can write well, and still another who's a computer nut. Match your tasks with the skills of the people in your charge.

Unfamiliar tasks. No sense wasting your time with a task someone else may be more suited to handle.

There are some tasks, however, that you shouldn't delegate:

Ceremonial tasks. Retirements, funerals, banquets, weddings, departmental celebrations, award ceremonies, and the like require your presence because of what you represent as well as who you are. Be there.

Personal tasks. Unless as a manager you are also a member of a team that evaluates its own performance, you want to make the final decisions about hiring, firing, and promoting.

Crises. Crises are inevitable but, by delegating effectively, you put yourself in a position to anticipate crises better and resolve them more quickly.

When you delegate, you not only help others grow, you grow too. A task that has become boring for you may not be boring for someone else. A task that has been done only by you should be taught to someone who can do it in your absence. To help you decide which tasks to delegate:

- Make a list of all your duties, including the time it takes you to complete each one.
- Makes a list of all the people on your staff, including their best skills and personal preferences.
- Match the duties with the people, including what additional training each staff member may require.
- Create a system to evaluate and measure your subordinates as they work to complete the assignments you delegated.

When assigning tasks, start with the people at the lowest levels of responsibility and work upward. And don't just assign any task, *sell* it. Explain to your chosen worker what's in this treasure: more challenging work, greater recognition, a break from routine, the possibility for advancement, the attention of higher-ups, the opportunity to learn new skills. Use the tasks you delegate as a way to establish support and create energy.

How you delegate a task is just as important as what you delegate and to whom. In other words, your attitude toward your workers greatly influences their willingness to respond and the quality of the work they do. Respect your workers, give them credit for their accomplishments, and show them why they've been chosen over all others. Knowing they're appreciated and are being given an opportunity to contribute in a more meaningful and significant way means more to most workers than an increase in salary, providing the pay they currently receive adequately covers their living expenses.

So give your delegatee the courtesy of a private conference. Schedule a time and place where you won't be interrupted. To ensure a successful delegation conference:

Prepare. Know why the task you're assigning and the person you've chosen are a good match, consider what you know about the delegatee to motivate her to do a good job, anticipate any questions she may ask, schedule enough time for the adequate discussion of any task, be prepared to provide whatever materials, resources, or training might be needed to complete the assignment, and clarify all levels of authority and responsibility. Most people left to their own devices will do too little rather than too much.

Present the desired results. Then channel your discussion into the methods needed to complete the task. Whenever possible, avoid the words "can't do" and rely as much as you can on your subordinate to discover her own methods.

Consider also stating the results you expect. Most people will work harder to fulfill the higher expectations of others than they will to meet their own. But be careful of what you expect. If your expectations are too low, your subordinate will become bored and will not be motivated; if your expectations are too high, your delegatee will become frustrated and give up quickly. Stretch your workers but don't break them.

Treat your delegatee as an equal. Your attitude should be one of team members working together to create a plan for what needs to be done.

Set a timetable. If possible, allow the delegatee to establish her own specific deadlines for completing the project. "Specific" is the key word here: "by the fifteenth of next month" is more effective than "sometime around the middle of the month."

A timetable also gives you the opportunity to to monitor the delegatee's progress and provide feedback.

Make your delegatee a star. Proudly introduce the person you've chosen to your supervisor, colleagues, and others working on the project. Make sure that everyone knows you've delegated your authority to this person and that she now has the power to resolve whatever problems might arise. Emphasizing the delegatee's authority reemphasizes her responsibilities and contributes to her confidence and self-esteem.

Solicit a firm commitment. "Can I count on you to have this investigation concluded and your report submitted by the fifteenth?" strengthens commitment more than a delegate's mere acceptance of a task. So does shaking hands at the end of the conference.

Let go. Once you've given your authority to someone else, honor it and your delegatee by not interfering. Not every task will be done as well as you could do it, but the person who learns from her mistakes will be better off (and so will you) than the one who's never given a chance to try. Support and confirm the wisdom of your choice as often as possible.

Be aware of reverse delegation. This occurs the first time your delegatee hits a serious snag and then hits you with "We've got a problem." When this happens, thrust the responsibility of solving the problem back onto the delegatee's shoulders. Avoid repeating your subordinate's use of the word "we." "You're right. There is a problem. What do you suggest?" Asking questions at this point is often more effective than providing answers.

If your delegatee lacks confidence, review the person's history of past accomplishments and how suitable she is for the task. If your delegatee is afraid of criticism, make sure your feedback is positively stated. In other words, get that "but" out of your mouth (e.g., "You're doing well, but . . ."). "But" just negates all that came before it. Change your "but" to an "and" (e.g., "You're doing well, and here's something else to consider: . . . ."). Above all, avoid the temptation to respond to your feeling of being needed. It's a powerful draw but one that is quickly discerned by your delegatee, who will use it to undermine both of you.

Accept responsibility. If your champion fails, admit that you made a poor choice, expected too much, didn't provide sufficient resources, didn't follow through as you should have, or whatever. Delegation is a risk that has to be taken *before* any benefits can be realized.

A final word about delegation: When you let go of your control and authority, you free yourself to seek new challenges and take on new responsibilities. You also help your subordinates grow with the new responsibilities you've assigned them. How much and how quickly you and your workers develop depends on how well you've prepared to delegate and what risks everyone involved is willing to take.

31

How to
Give and
Take Criticism

This chapter would never have been written if we'd been taught as children to view criticism as an opportunity to learn more about ourselves, as a means to make us more effective, as a technique for identifying deficiencies that we can work on correcting, as the natural outcome of not being able to please everybody, as a measurement for meeting standards, as a guide for bringing our abilities in line with our achievements, as the possible difference between success and failure, and as a benefit that only a fool wouldn't take full advantage of.

Unfortunately, our self-images are in large part determined by how others see us and, when we're not viewed as we think we should be, we become confused, upset, frustrated, and angry. To use the viewpoints of others to our advantage, we need to think and respond differently to the criticism we receive.

To think differently about any criticism, remember that you control how you view yourself. When you allow others to make you feel diminished, and if you believe the negative criticism you receive is an indication of failure, you diminish yourself. Worse, you begin erecting defenses to protect yourself and, in the process, create a prison of stagnation and death. Or you take the negative viewpoints of others to heart and see yourself as a failure. Once you see yourself as a failure, it's only a matter of time before you are one.

Just because you're not perfect doesn't mean you aren't effective; just because someone is rude or inconsiderate doesn't mean that you said or did something offensive; just because your last interview didn't turn out as well as you had hoped doesn't mean the next one will; just because you made a mistake doesn't mean you're an idiot; just because your proposal wasn't accepted doesn't mean you're a failure. What these mean is that anyone can make a mistake, someone other than you can have a bad day, and that any setback is temporary and can be turned into a valuable learning experience. If you can accept rejection and welcome criticism as vehicles for improvement, the less stressed and more motivated you will become. So turn rejection and criticism to your advantage. These things are only negative because you've been taught to see them that way.

How to Respond to Criticism

Because you control the meaning you attach to criticism, you also control how you respond to it. Here are some tips on how to respond to the negative viewpoints of others:

Listen (see pp. 81–85). Listening is the hardest part— especially if the criticism is accurate. Resist the temptation to interrupt or counterattack, accept all that's fair, and don't undermine your receptivity with counterproductive body language.

Respond positively. Thank the person for bringing the matter to your attention or, if the criticism is inaccurate, acknowledge the time and effort your critic took to make you aware of his opinion.

Ask questions. Asking questions is especially important if your critic is either aggressive or passive. Questions enable the aggressive critic to vent anger and the reticent critic to overcome any timidity he might have.

Your questions should lead your critic to specific answers. Use her adjectives and adverbs as springboards for further questions ("What did I do, specifically, that was "irresponsible'?").

And be aware of the tone in your voice. If your questions come across as sarcastic, you've not only lost your chance of solving the problem, you've also created an atmosphere where communication is difficult and any hope of building a better relationship with your critic becomes seriously damaged.

Assess. If the criticism is valid, accept the fact that you're not perfect, apologize for your mistake, and assure your critic it won't be repeated.

If the criticism is not valid, the reason may well be that you didn't live up to your critic's expectations. Having constructed a false image of who you are, your critic expected you to act a certain way in a given situation and, when you didn't, she was disappointed. This is not your fault— unless you helped create the false image. Either way your response is the same: ask questions requiring specific answers so you can discover your critic's expectations. Then learn how the false image was created and compile the information you'll need to make a relevant response or take appropriate action.

If your critic cannot respond to your questions in specific terms, chances are the issue or behavior being critiqued is a cover for more deep-seated feelings: jealousy, insecurity, envy, misplaced competiveness, fear of failure.

Although this behavior suggests more about your critic than it does about you, it's still a problem you have to deal with. Channel your questions into a discussion that will lead the two of you to any underlying causes, watch the nonverbal behavior of your critic, and allow the intensity of his feelings to determine what actions you want to take now and what ones you want to take later.

Acknowledge. The most effective way to handle valid criticism is to take responsibility for what you did. This doesn't mean, however, that you have to put yourself down or bring up a litany of your shortcomings. Admit your mistake and, if you think helpful, ask your critic for suggestions on how to improve your performance. Now you're focusing on solutions instead of feeling guilty or incompetent.

If the criticism is vague and your critic has difficulty being specific about the issue, acknowledge the possibility that some of what he says may be true (e.g., "You might be right about that . . ." or "I think you've got a point there. Let me ask you . . . ."). This technique, known as "fogging," keeps you in the role of the listener and allows you to judge if the criticism is accurate.

If the criticism is unjustified, you can ignore it, but you should respond to your critic. Remaining silent is to appear guilty, threaten your self-confidence, and risk losing the respect of others. A better approach is to disagree tactfully or ask additional questions to unearth your critic's true feelings. If you can't use the information your critic offers, at least you exhaust your critic's complaints. If you're patient (read: keep finding ways to listen), you may discover a common ground upon which to build a better relationship for the future.

Take time out. For the criticism that is vague, unjustified, or requires a more thoughtful response than an apology and the promise not to repeat your mistake, ask your critic to give you some time to think about what he or she said. This prevents you from saying something you'll regret, gives you time to decide how you want to act, doesn't respond negatively to your critic and, because it provides the two of you with some time to calm down, allows you to be more objective in your approach for a solution and your critic to be more receptive to whatever you suggest.

Respond. Admit where you're wrong, apologize for your mistakes, and suggest a course of action to prevent your error from reoccurring. Where you disagree, agree to disagree and, if you think it would help strengthen your relationship, suggest further discussions of the matter.

Act. The most effective way to change a critic's attitude toward you is to change your behavior. Don't waste your time formulating excuses or rationalizing what you did. Actions speak louder than words. If your critic is correct, show him how serious you are about avoiding similar mistakes and begin acting in ways that differ noticeably from your previous behavior.

If You Must be Negative, Do It Positively

We carry just as many negative messages of criticism now as we did when we were children: the problem will resolve itself if you just leave it alone; you're not perfect, don't expect others to be; you don't enjoy being criticized, no one else does either; you have no right to judge; it's easier to do it yourself; anything you say will just be held against you; you should have said something earlier, now you're too angry to calm down; you criticize people and they're not going to like you; nothing good can come from saying bad things about a person; keep your negative feelings to yourself.

Criticism doesn't have to be bad, however. Well thought-out, sensitively presented criticism can correct repeated mistakes, improve job performance, discourage the playing of mind games, reduce stress, encourage honesty, correct people's unrealistic expectations, increase productivity, promote growth, boost morale, and lay the foundation for a relationship built on openess and trust.

To deliver the kind of criticism that will be welcomed:

Look at yourself first. Are your expectations of the person you're about to criticize realistic or based on a false image you created? Have you ever discussed with this person your expectations of the goals and levels of achievement you expected her to meet? Have you provided your subordinate with frequent feedback on his or her performance? If you've never discussed these matters, what is the basis of your criticism? Is your criteria for evaluation fair? If you have discussed the matter of goals and expectations and provided frequent feedback, chances are that the person you're planning to criticize will already have a clear idea of what you're talking about, will be receptive to any suggestions you might make, and will be more likely to respond in ways that will benefit you both.

Time your criticism. Unless the person you need to talk to is under pressure from another source, you should express your feedback as closely as possible to the event you wish to criticize. Don't be the kind of manager who only notices when something goes wrong. Praise your subordinates many more times than you criticize them. In fact, some serious helpings of consistent praise can go a long way toward softening the blow of negative criticism.

Raise the issue. Avoid accusations and defensive responses by using "I" statements (e.g., "I need your help with . . . ." "I feel concerned when . . . . "). Use open-ended questions to discover how your subordinate sees the situation (e.g., "Why do you think this is happening?"), and repeat your correspondent's viewpoint to make sure there is no misunderstanding (e.g., "So you think . . . ").

Be specific. Avoid adjectives such as "irresponsible," "unprepared," "unreliable," adverbs such as "badly," "poorly," and absolute adjectives and adverbs such as "worst," "always," "never." Describe the action or behavior in specific, concrete terms (i.e., time, date, place) and delay any discussion of motive or goals. That's your subordinate's responsibility.

Continue to use "I" statements. "You" statements blame your correspondent and make her feel diminished or defensive. "I" statements enable you to acknowledge your feelings without personally attacking your subordinate (e.g., "I feel frustrated when I have to . . ." as opposed to "You let me down"). "I" also takes responsibility for your emotions, prevents empowering your subordinate with the ability to make you feel pain or anger, and lets your listener know the effect her behavior (not personality) has on you.

Seek a change in behavior. Don't be satisfied with an apology and a promise it won't happen again. Give the person you're criticizing an opportunity to act on your feedback instead of just feeling guilty or diminished in some other way that may harbor resentment. Ask for her suggestions (e.g., "How do you think we can avoid this in the future?").

End on a positive note. Affirm your subordinate's ability to change, show confidence in her by describing the benefits that can be expected, and offer to help implement any of the changes that have been agreed on.

Follow up. A follow-up allows you and your subordinate to share a sense of accomplishment and closure. If the plan of action hasn't been carried out, your correspondent won't be surprised if the issue has resurfaced, and you will be able to confirm in his or her mind the seriousness of the matter by following the exact same procedures that have already been described.

If you correspondent's counterproductive behavior persists, arrange for a special conference. Ask yourself, "If my way is so good, why hasn't my subordinate changed her behavior? What's the reason for her feelings?" These questions should help you determine the sources and intensity of your subordinate's resistance to change. When you've reached your conclusions, consider these techniques for being more persuasive:

Ask for less that you expect. Perhaps the change would be best handled in smaller, incremental steps.

Focus on the issue, not the person. Avoid making conclusions that can't be drawn from your subordinate's stated viewpoints or specific behavior.

Show you understand. Rephrase and repeat your subordinate's thoughts and feelings in your own words. Work with what's familiar to her rather than what's obvious to you. Show you respect the opposing opinions and take them seriously.

Look for areas of agreement. Show how your solutions coincide with the issues you've already agreed on; demonstrate the losses that may be suffered if the necessary changes don't take place.

Stick to simple claims. Usually, the more simple the claim, the more ways there are to restate it. Be enthusiastic but not overbearing. Try to sell rather force the issue. Use the kind of sentences and tones of voice that you would be most receptive to.

Encourage your subordinate to ask questions. Who knows? There might be more to this problem than meets your eye.

Ask for a plan of action. One that is specific, reasonable, and measurable. Make sure your subordinate knows what has to be done, how it has to be done, and when it has to be done.

Get a commitment. Ask your correspondent, "Can I count on you to . . . by . . . ?" But don't expect your subordinate to change overnight. Your ability to persuade is not measured by your intelligence and effort; it has more to do with your subordinate's attitudes, beliefs, and ingrained patterns of behavior. Relationships are complex, which is only one of the reasons why managing is so difficult.

A Final Note on Giving Criticism

If given the choice, deliver your negative criticism in person and your positive criticism in person and in writing. Don't present negative criticism in writing until you feel the time has come to start keeping a record of your subordinate's substandard behavior. Aside from contributing to a record, the primary advantage of written criticism is that you avoid a face-to-face confrontation. A written criticism, however, is a permanent record and can be used against you if your message isn't accurate or your tone is inappropriate. Written critiques can also be refuted point-by-point and cause you to spend more time and energy on the matter than it's worth.

If you decide to write a letter, check carefully the accuracy of your claim, make sure your tone of voice is objective and reinforces your reasons for wanting to solve the problem, cite specific examples (preferably ones you've already discussed so you won't blindside your reader), and end on a positive note by affirming the value you place on the person you're criticizing.

32

How to Motivate Others

One key to motivating workers is to give them what they want. And what do workers want? In a study by Rutgers University, employees were given a list of 10 job factors and asked to rank the importance of each from 1 to 10. A group of managers was given the same list and asked to rank the same factors as they thought the employees would.

The managers' ranking top three: raises, promotion, job security.

The employees' top three: respect, personal growth, and freedom to express their opinions, followed by consideration for the individual, appreciation for work that is well done, and accurate information about company policies and decisions.

Ironically, both the managers and the employees were right. Had the employees not been making enough money to house and feed their families, their first choices probably would have been financial. Abraham Maslow tells us that all people (even those who don't work for a living) seek to satisfy five different needs:

Survival needs. Food, sleep, and shelter are the basic survival needs.

Security needs. Money in the bank, insurance, and job security are the security needs.

Belonging needs. People want to belong to and be accepted by a group. Our families are our primary group; the people we work with form another. Managers who frown on "socializing" at work take note: you're depriving your workers of a basic human need and depriving yourselves of a valuable resource.

Prestige needs. People want to know their contributions are appreciated. When they're not, they burn out and turn off.

169

Self-fulfillment needs. Because so many people spend so much of their time trying to be accepted, appreciated, and rewarded, they don't often get around to participating in the kinds of activities that please us in a personal (what Maslow calls "self-actualizing") way. Happy were the cavepeople who sang, danced, and painted their dwellings with animals.

Once employees satisfy their lower needs (survival and security), they start searching to meet the other needs (e.g., belonging, prestige, and self-fulfillment). Employees, however, can be at different levels at different times and at more than one level at the same time. People who feel threatened by the rumor of a layoff, for example, may be responding to needs on the survival level (i.e., "How am I going to feed my family?") while attempting to secure their positions on the prestige level.

But the rumor of layoffs is not the problem facing most workers. The biggest problem for most employees is their employers. The two — employees and employers — are usually at odds with one another. While employers focus on production and profit, employees want more attention paid to their human needs. A them-against-us attitude quickly develops, and employees who once worked hard and behaved responsibly are labeled "difficult."

Here are some of the characteristics of these difficult people:

- They prefer to think for themselves than do what they're told.
- They don't think their bosses are right because their bosses are the bosses.
- They want work to be fun or at least have some fun at work.
- They think they know some better ways to run things.
- They resent not being listened to and get bored when they're not challenged.
- They're not content to work without understanding the big picture or seeing the end result of their efforts.
- They want to be rewarded for their accomplishments.

Sound familiar? It should, because these needs are perfectly normal. To provide your subordinates with less is to reduce them to functionaries or worse.

To give your subordinates what they need to become fully realized human beings and, at the same time, to motivate them to produce at higher and more effective levels:

Inform. Give your subordinates the big picture. Let them see the end result of their efforts. The more information an employee has about the company's goals, the more they feel a part of the company and the better equipped they are to act in the company's best interests.

So know what you're talking about and don't confuse facts with opinions. Your subordinates want to depend on you and their company to be open, honest, knowledgeable, and forthcoming with the information they need to get on with the jobs they were hired to do. Uninformed employees never feel as if they belong and spend a lot of time and energy not getting involved in their work and keeping their eyes open for other jobs. Informed employees don't have to depend on a "grapevine" and can focus on meeting their objectives.

Delegate. (see pp. 157–161) Delegate tasks authority. Unless the person assigned the task is also in charge of it, there has been no delegation. So help your delegatee by removing any barriers that may be in his way. Making sure everyone concerned knows the delegatee's levels of authority and responsibility is one way of doing this. Another is not to interfere once the delegation has been made.

Praise. Because so many workers complain their work is only noticed when a mistake has been made, you, as manager, want to give plenty of positive feedback. Praise your employee in public; save your negative responses for private conversations.

Listen (see pp. 81–85). Don't interrupt, don't jump to conclusions, don't diagnose, and don't offer advice until you've been asked for it. Even then, you should respond with questions to help your correspondent discover for himself what needs to be known. Do, however, give information, provide emotional support, and avoid saying things like, "You're doing a good job; don't blow it."

Reward. Recognizing effort and accomplishment boosts production as well as morale. It also builds confidence, instills loyalty, and motivates people to take greater risks.

Consider these rewards for lower-level employees:

- a cash bonus
- a parking space for a month
- a trophy where everyone can see it
- a note in the company newsletter
- a nomination for Employee of the Year
- a lunch with the president of the company
- a picture on the bulletin board of the employee shaking hands with the president outside of the restaurant where they had lunch
- a written note of appreciation from you
- a dinner for two at a local restaurant or theatre tickets or both

And here are some rewards for the higher-ups:

- a cash bonus or raise or both
- a promotion or formal recognition

- a day off with pay
- a paid membership in a professional organization or subscription to a professional journal
- an increase in benefits
- profit-sharing, or incentives
- a dinner for two and tickets to the theatre
- a sabbatical or paid vacation.

Rewards, especially financial ones, can backfire if the recipient feels the recognition is not genuine or is a substitute for what the recipient really deserves (a promotion, for example).

To ensure effective recognition, demonstrate consistent, genuine concern on a daily basis: know and call your subordinates by their names, know the names of their spouses and children and ask about them, handwrite notes of appreciation (for work well done) and congratulations (a promotion, wedding, child's graduation). Leave an occasional reward when your subordinate least expects it: a card, a bouquet of flowers, a lunch, tickets to a show or concert, an afternoon off from work.

Train. Tuition for a course at the local college, a day-long workshop, or expense-paid attendance at a conference in another city boosts morale as does the offer to provide cross-training. Training also helps reduce boredom, defuse tension, heighten creativity, and increase production.

Make work interesting. Add interest to the job by rearranging work flows, creating flex time, discussing your production problems with your subordinates, creating opportunities for group discussions, making sure everyone understands the significance of their contribution to the end product, and developing an atmosphere where meaningful communication can take place without the fear of reprisal.

Make work fun. Encourage employees to publish a newsletter, adopt a highway, represent a charity, form a company sports team, and throw a company party at a local restaurant or hotel.

Value. Employees usually know more than managers about how things work (look to them for ways to improve procedures), and they often have more diverse backgrounds than managers (because they've often held more jobs, they frequently know more ways of doing things).

Reward their suggestions with a notice on the departmental bulletin board, in the company newsletter, in a congratulatory flyer, or with an acknowledgement at a group or company meeting. Write a personal letter of appreciation and praise (not on company stationery) to your contributing subordinate and then write a similar letter to her family.

Care. The more you care for your subordinates, the more they'll care for your company's clients and customers. So treat them as professional colleagues. Greet them genuinely, warmly, and enthusiastically; ask them questions and take time to listen to their answers. Solicit their advice involve them in discussions, treat them fairly and with respect, emphasize their importance to the team, department, and company, praise their efforts, reward their accomplishments, assess and fulfill their needs, judge their behavior but not their character, respond quickly to their needs, and provide whatever opportunities you can for growth and development.

That should keep you busy and most of your efforts will be rewarded. How soon depends on the history of motivation at your company, the attitude of your subordinates, and how genuinely concerned and helpful you are.

An Alternative to Maslow

David McClelland differs from Maslow in this sense: Whereas Maslow claims that most of the needs in his hierarchy are innate, McClelland holds that most of our needs are learned and may vary from one culture to another. Rather than trying to satisfy the basic needs of people, as Maslow suggests, McClelland insists that we discover and work to satisfy our workers' individual needs. Fortunately, there are only three: affiliation, power, and achievement.

Affiliation

People whose needs fall into the affiliation category focus most of their time and energy on relationships. They often seek the approval of others, bond with people who share their views, want to be liked by most of the members in any group, and try to resolve tensions that might exist among the people they know.

According to McClelland, people with strong affiliation needs work best in situations where they're helping others: teaching, coaching, customer service, coordinating people in jobs or departments, or integrating goals with various people in a department or company.

Power

People with power needs like to win. More concerned with persuading and prevailing rather than negotiating and accepting, power people are determined to have their own way in everything. For them, life is a series of win-lose confrontations. For you (if you marry, live with, or work for one) the happy life is loyalty, devotion, and obedience. What you gain for what you give up (and many do it willingly) is a sense of security, that you will be taken care of. It's a false sense of security, but it is a sense of security nevertheless.

Power people can lead their followers to higher levels of achievement and competence, but these followers are always controlled by their leaders. That's the trade-off: you gain but never on your own and only so far as you're allowed.

Power people work best in situations calling for strong leadership and the attainment of goals. It's the power people who, if they don't get burned out by the constant competition, often make it to the top in any organizational setting.

Achievement

Achievement people are not intimidated by problems, accept responsibility for their behavior, are willing to take calculated risks, and welcome feedback— positive and negative. People with high achievement needs become doctors, lawyers, accountants, engineers, computer specialists, sales representatives, and the owners of their own small businesses. These people don't need to be motivated.

The biggest challenge for managers in the McClelland school of thought is to match the right person with the right job. Once you have a match, the individual's affiliation, power, or achievement needs will do the rest. Or most of it.

Making any match difficult, however, is the fact that a person with high needs in one area may not have low needs in the other two. This combination of needs is further complicated by the degrees to which people vary in their energy levels, positive and negative viewpoints, and other factors of conditioning.

In the long run, none of Maslow's nor McClelland's principles can maintain motivation for very long. They can help people get started or get them back on track or even keep them going a while longer, but they can't sustain any energy unless the individual is self-motivated. Help your subordinates clarify their goals, focus on completing their tasks, reward their efforts, and provide opportunities for growth. Match them with the right assignments and free them to accomplish what they require to satisfy their personal needs (innate and learned) and you've done a lot.

33

How to Conduct Win-Win Reviews

The subordinate's name is on your appraisal form; the subordinate's performance is being appraised; the subordinate's security, advancement, and income are at stake. Be fair (judge your employee on criteria that determine success, not your own biases or prejudices) and be honest. Dishonest negative appraisals cause reduced satisfaction, motivation, and commitment; dishonest positive appraisals cause lessened effort, inflated expectations, and false senses of accomplishment and security. Make sure your reviews are also timely (to encourage success and prevent failure) and thorough (the employee has the right to know exactly where she stands).

Before the Appraisal Meeting

Review your subordinate's performance. Check your subordinate's file for any pertinent notes or memos, confer with your supervisor about her evaluation of your subordinate's performance, and make notes on whatever you wish to discuss at the appraisal conference so you won't forget anything.

Schedule a meeting. Consider meeting somewhere other than your office, allow more time than you need, make sure you won't be interrupted and, if you have to meet in your office, plan to sit somewhere other than behind your desk. You don't want your subordinate to feel rushed by your schedule, less important than any phone call, or intimidated by the authority your desk might symbolize.

Prepare your subordinate. Give your subordinate a copy of your appraisal form or a list of the issues you plan to discuss at the performance. Allowing your subordinate to participate enhances her self-esteem, gives her a sense of control, and underscores the idea that the appraisal conference should be of mutual benefit.

Plan an agenda. Whatever the issues you wish to discuss, you want to open the appraisal conference by making sure your subordinate understands that the review is a mutual process, not a report card. The two of you will determine how well your correspondent completed the tasks in her job description as well as what additional responsibilities she will assume. Save any discussion of money for a separate conference; this one is for performance.

Let your subordinate begin the appraisal discussion. To confirm the point that the conference is a mutual process, ask your correspondent to present her assessment first. Allowing your subordinate to conduct a self-evaluation also reduces any tendencies for her to be defensive and provides you with the opportunity to discuss your correspondent's short-comings without having to introduce them. Because your responding to the issues of poor performance that your subordinate already raised, she should be more willing to listen to what you have to say.

Respond immediately. Because you want a mutually beneficial conference, be careful of what you say and how you say it. Your first response, therefore, should confirm the positive things your subordinate said about herself. Back up what you say with some specific examples based on your own observations or reports from others. Make sure your correspondent knows you appreciate what she did and encourage your subordinate to keep up the good work.

Consider disagreeing with at least one of your correspondent's negative evaluations and support your statement with specific examples. If your subordinate doesn't at first agree with you, cite another example to prove your point. Again encourage your correspondent to continue what she is doing well.

Next bring up any instance of poor performance your subordinate raised. Say that you agree with her self-estimation, show how the poor performance affects others, and ask your correspondent if she has considered any measures to resolve the problem. Because your subordinate introduced the issue, chances are she will have some suggestions for resolving it. Listen carefully and watch for any contradicting facial expressions or body language. Summarizing what your correspondent has said should eliminate any doubts or identify any misunderstanding.

Support whatever suggestions your subordinate makes, add what you can to make them more effective, and offer to work with your correspondent to create a plan of specific actions to correct the problem. Make sure the plan is measurable and includes a timetable for reporting and evaluating.

Finally, you want to introduce any areas where you think your subordinate needs to improve. Be polite and sensitive, support your conclusions with specific examples, and ask your correspondent if she agrees with your assessment. If not, cite additional examples from your own observation, your subordinate's file, and the opinions of others. Once you have agreement, suggest some of the ways you've been thinking of to resolve the problem and work together on an effective action plan.

Summarize. Begin your summary with your subordinate's accomplishments and move on to the plans the two of you have created to improve performance. Don't waste time with the negative and the past; focus on the positive, the present, and the future.

Follow up. Reward your subordinate as soon as you see performance improving, show how the improved performance has helped others, encourage your subordinate to continue to do good work, and ask if there is anything you can do to maintain the new level of achievement.

And don't stop! Your subordinate needs your feedback (positive and negative) so adjustments can be made. Don't wait for a formal conference; emphasize your willingness to participate daily in open communication. This, not any formal appraisal, is the foundation of good relationships. It also makes appraisal conferences easier if you and your subordinate have been working on whatever issues are scheduled for discussion.

What to Do If You're the One Being Reviewed

The challenge for the person being reviewed is establishing and maintaining control of a situation in which the other person has all or most of the power.

Two things to do:

Prepare. Prepare at least twice as much and twice as hard as the person reviewing you. Read the chapters in this book on listening (pp. 81–85), giving and receiving criticism (pp. 162–168), handling difficult people (pp. 148–152), and win-win negotiation (pp. 106–109). While reading these chapters, take notes on the points pertaining to your relationship with the reviewer. Then create an agenda of what you want to say and how, according to your notes, you want to say it.

Create. Using the suggestions in this chapter as a model, create an action plan for conducting your own performance review.

Review your performance. Go through your personnel file for any relevant memos, letters of congratulation, and certificates of completion for any courses or workshops you may have attended. Ask supervisors who won't be reviewing you but are familiar with your work to give their opinion of your performance. Any patterns in their responses might be clues as to what issues your reviewer might raise. Prepare responses for these issues as well as for anything in your file that might be used against you.

Schedule a meeting. Agree to meet your reviewer at a time that will give you an opportunity to discuss all the items on both your agendas. If your reviewer is not aware that your performance appraisal is a two-way communication process, you're going to need even more time.

Ask for a copy of your company's appraisal form. Then fill it out as if you were your manager reviewing you. See yourself from his perspective. If your company doesn't have a standard form, ask your reviewer what topics he thinks will be most important to discuss.

Take control early. If you can introduce the topics for discussion, you have more control over what will be said about those subjects, especially if you've prepared to present them from the viewpoint of your reviewer. Accept responsibility for your behavior, avoid pointing a finger at others, and emphasize your accomplishments. Stress what you've learned from any mistakes you made.

If your reviewer feels obligated to find some area for you to improve in (and most think they're not doing their job if they don't), listen without interrupting, ask questions of clarification that require specific answers, acknowledge where you made your mistakes, and ask for suggestions to improve in these areas. For what you disagree with or are not sure about, ask for time to consider the criticism and request a follow-up conference.

Even though what you talk about may be clear to you, be sure to ask for a copy of your reviewer's appraisal. Then, when you respond in a letter to be placed with your review in your personnel file, use specific details to refute the conclusions you disagree with, mention the specific steps you've already taken to correct the mistakes you've made in the past, and end on a positive note. Mention your appreciation for the feedback, the opportunity to respond, and how much you look forward to your continued association with the company.

34

How to
Hire and Fire

Whether you hire or fire, your goal as a manager is to achieve win-win results. Hiring doesn't have as much to do with finding the top candidate for the job as deciding which candidate has the behavior and technical skills most suited to the job. An underqualified person with a vision and some energy, for example, may be a better choice than someone with more experience. And the more success we have matching jobs with candidates, the fewer the problems we'll experience later on. Not to have much experience in firing people is a credit to your hiring ability but, if you someday have to fire someone, it's best for you and the person being terminated to be prepared. If the firing comes as a surprise to the employee, you failed as a manager.

How to Hire

Determine the necessary skills. Make a list of the tasks required by the job and what skills (technical and behavior) are necessary to complete these tasks. You may want a secretary, for example, who is computer literate, has strong editing skills, is good on the telephone, and likes to help customers. Finding a candidate who can work on a computer and edit is relatively easy (most people can be coached on how to answer the phone); but it's very difficult to train someone to like to work with other people. So in your advertisement for the position and your interviews, you want to hire the candidate who possesses the skills that are most difficult to teach. This person may not be the fastest typist but, if he or she can adequately complete the tasks requiring technical skills and is obviously a "people person," you've found your match.

Decide how you want to search for your candidate. If you promote from within the company, you reward someone for work well done but you run the risk of causing dissension, especially if you're filling a supervisory position and the person you select will be managing former peers. If you advertise for someone outside of the company, you will bring in someone with a different perspective but who is unfamiliar with the company's vision, policies, products, and procedures (read: money and time spent on training).

If a personnel department is conducting the job search, make sure your contact knows exactly what you're looking for, the job description is updated and accurate, and you've discussed fully what the position entails with the company's screener.

Another source for finding candidates is your network of friends and colleagues. To create the widest and deepest pool of applicants, however, pursue all of the alternatives. You'll increase your chances of success and reduce your risk of problems developing after a person has been hired.

Prepare a list of questions you want to ask the candidates chosen for an interview. Avoid the kinds of questions that seem as if they were lifted from a book on how to interview job applicants. Your candidate, if he has half a brain, will probably have some answers prepared. Questions such as these include: "What can you tell us about yourself?" "What's your worst feature?" "Where do you see yourself five years from now?"

To test the efficacy of your questions, try answering them yourself, do it extemporaneously, the way your candidate has to.

- What do you like best about your job?
- Why do you want to leave it?
- What could you have done differently on your last job?
- What's the most interesting project you ever worked on?
- Describe the best boss you ever had.
- What do you like to do in your spare time?
- What's the last good book you read?
- Do you have any role models?
- Describe a conflict you resolved.

- What do you think is your greatest accomplishment?

Also ask the same questions of each candidate so you can compare answers, but don't stick so closely to the script that you miss an opportunity to explore an interesting line of thought.

Conduct the interview. Welcome the candidate, do what you can to make him feel at ease, explain the agenda for the interview, be sure to give the job applicant an opportunity to ask you questions.

An interview is a meeting, and your candidate has the right to see if he wants to work with you. Again, it's the match that's important, not who wins or loses.

Avoid any questions relating to age, sex, race, religion, color, nationality, citizenship, disabilities, marriage, and arrests. Unless these questions are asked as part of an affirmative action program, they violate a candidate's civil rights.

Make notes. After each interview, take five minutes to jot down your reactions to the applicant. This helps you remember the candidate and helps the candidate be remembered.

Follow up. Check the candidate's references, confer with others who participated in the selection process, reach a consensus, telephone the successful candidate, and write a sensitive letter to the applicants who were not selected, including those who were not interviewed.

How to Fire

If you've done your job as a manager, your subordinate will not only expect to be fired, he may very well be relieved to have it finally over with. Both you and your subordinate should know and feel that the terminated person is not a bad person. He is just not right for this job. Now this person has the opportunity to find a job better suited to his skills and personality.

There are only two reasons why someone should be fired: they can't do the work (regardless of how much training they might have had) or they can't get along with others (regardless of the counselling they may have received).

By the time a termination conference is scheduled, you should have spoken informally with your subordinate at the first sign of a problem, follow up this conversation with others in which you and your subordinate discussed ways to resolve the problem, reached more than a few agreements to improve the situation, documented in writing several formal conferences, and carefully monitored your subordinate's efforts to fulfill the terms of your agreement.

Keeping an employee at this point doesn't do you, your subordinate, or your company much good. You are wasting your time trying to improve your subordinate's performance, the employee is wasting time in a position for which he is ill-suited, other employees can see that their sub standard colleague is not pulling his weight (so why should they?), and you're all draining your company's resources.

To make any termination meeting as painless as possible:

Know what you're going to say. Focus on the facts of your subordinate's performance or behavior. Rely on the records you kept and avoid words such as "irresponsible" and "unreliable." They imply a value judgment.

Keep the meeting short. Set a time limit and stick to it; the longer the meeting continues, the more likely you'll say something you'll wish you hadn't.

Act decisively. Make your message clear and firm so there are no misunderstandings or false hopes. But also be considerate of your subordinate's feelings. Even when the employee knows his firing is imminent, the rejection and humiliation still hurts.

Put yourself in the place of your subordinate, treat him as you would like to be treated, and leave your correspondent with the feeling that you've provided an opportunity he knew was necessary. Able to continue his career along a different path, your subordinate will probably be grateful to you for what you did even though the pain of termination will never go away.

Ask the employee if he would prefer to resign rather than be fired (this saves face but eliminates unemployment compensation) and ask your former subordinate what his colleagues should be told.

Follow up. Although you don't want your subordinate to continue working after he has been fired (the risk of his affecting the morale of others is too great), it's a good idea to invite the now former employee to attend an exit interview. This is usually conducted by someone in the personnel department. It concerns issues such as severance pay, retirement benefits, unemployment compensation, profit-sharing premiums, suggestions and possibly training for another job, and a discussion about what the company might do to prevent similar firings in the future.

Consider telephoning your former subordinate six months after the termination. Chances are he will have found another job as well as a more objective perspective on what happened and why. Perhaps something he says might indicate a weakness in the hiring process that can be corrected. If you can improve your hiring practices, you'll have performed a service for everyone who will ever be an employee of your company.

35

How to Create Self-Managed Work Teams

Self-managed work teams are being created because the traditional hierarchal power structure is no longer effective.

After World War II, the United States was an economic as well as a military power. Uncle Sam could produce more goods for less money and sell them cheaper than any other country and, because most of the rest of the world was in ruins, he had a ready market. As the economies of the devastated nations revived, especially in Germany and Japan, the companies in these countries realized they couldn't compete with America's large industrial giants.

So they created niches for themselves within the larger market with such products as smaller, more fuel-efficient cars. They also began producing better quality products: radios with clearer sound and televisions with sharper pictures. These companies also discovered that bigger was not necessarily better and took the calculator America invented and put it in people's pockets all over the world. Then they put in people's wallets. They created, improved, and changed products and markets so fast, few companies in the United States could keep up. "Made in the USA" replaced "Made in Japan" as the world's greatest symbol of junk.

How'd they do it? One of the ways was through self-managed or self-directed work teams. Taking an American idea that was rejected by United States' corporations after World War II, countries first in Asia and later in Europe flattened their traditional power hierarchies. They took decision-making authority away from those in management and gave it to teams formed by people who did the actual work. No longer would an idea have to be proposed to upper management, a study conducted, a report issued, a decision made, and an order given. By the time the idea traveled up the hierarchal ladder of power and returned as a directive, it was too late. Either the market or the technology or both had changed.

But teams do more than just save time. They also:

Create more solutions. A group of people working together as a team can think of more solutions and more barriers to those solutions than most people working by themselves.

Make better decisions. People who complete tasks often know more about them than those who assign the tasks. With teams, there's very little guessing about whether any given solution will work.

Increase commitment. If a team makes a decision and is responsible for its implementation, there's more at stake. Consequently, the team's members are more willing to work together to succeed.

Spread the responsibility. Workers on a team are not as individually accountable as they would be in a traditional power hierarchy. As a result, they're more willing to take risks.

Exploit resources. Team members challenge, communicate, inspire, debate, and bring out the best in each other. No longer are they quite so willing to fear action because they fear failure.

To create a self-managed team, however, is not easy or fast. The average time needed to turn a group of workers into a self-directed unit can take anywhere from two to three years. One of the obvious reasons for this is management's reluctance to give up power and change the definition of the roles they play, but workers also resist changing. Many of them are happy with the way things are, enjoy the privileges of seniority, feel they have enough responsibility as it is, and are afraid not just of the unknown (lost jobs?) but also of the known. What is the history of change at your company? Does your company take care of its workers during times of transition or insecurity?

Your first job in creating a self-managed work team, then, is to convince your subordinates how much more they have to gain by abandoning the traditional power hierarchy and participating in a self-directed work team. Furthermore, they have to learn fast and adopt quickly if they are to survive the constant changes in today's world.

But you, the manager, must also learn to love change because, as your subordinate's roles change from those held in the power hierarchy to those created by the self-directed team, so do yours. To create a successful team, you and your team members will have to complete four successive stages of learning:

1. *Unconscious incompetence.* At this stage, the team members don't know they're incompetent and don't see a need for change. Your job is to convince them that the old ways are no longer effective.

2. *Conscious incompetence.* Having successfully enlightened your subordinates of their incompetence, they will look to you for new, more effective ways to solve their problems and complete their tasks. Your answer? Self-managed work teams.

3. *Conscious competence.* At this stage, your subordinates have learned the team skills you've taught them, but they're not yet comfortable with them. They feel awkward and self-conscious. Now your role is no longer that of the traditional manager; now you shift into being a coach. Having taught them what to do, their job is to do it. Your job is to let them do it.

4. *Unconscious competence.* Now the skills you've taught your team members have become a habit, part of their natural behavior. Now your role has to change again. Your team no longer needs a coach; now it wants a facilitator or coordinator.

To lead yourself and your team members through these four stages of learning you will need all of the skills presented in this book. And you're going to need some help from upper management as well. If the people at the top don't support you and your team at every stage of its development, you will fail. Upper management, furthermore, has to complete some tasks of its own. It must support the team in action as well as words, provide whatever training and resources are necessary for the team to succeed, and eliminate any policies and structures that encourage hierarchal thinking. Who, for example, has offices with windows, keys to special bathrooms, and passwords to all the computers? Who are addressed by their first names and who by their last?

Let's take a closer look at each of the four stages of development that you, team leader and team player, have to lead yourself and your team members through. Each sequence contains a series of tasks that must be completed before the team can succeed at the next stage of its development. Sometimes the team will be in two stages at once. That's okay. Sometimes, given the time and energy you've devoted to a project, your team will regress further than you thought possible. That's okay too. Fear, panic, mistakes, and regression are not failure. They're fear, panic, mistakes, and regression. Be patient, repeat what works, correct what doesn't, and persevere. You're holding in your hands what you need to succeed.

Stage 1: Unconscious Incompetence

This stage, convincing your subordinates that the old ways are no longer effective, shouldn't be too difficult. Show them the big picture: Since 1987, 90 million American workers have been given permanent pink slips; of all the mergers that took place in the last decade (more than at any time in history), only 23 percent of them have been successful; the national work force during that same period was cut by more than 15 percent; the buyout rate is double today what it was three years ago; the last 100 takeovers affected almost four million workers; IBM, which once prided itself on never laying off anyone, fired thousands and put 47 percent of its property up for sale in less than a year.

Next, let your future team members know how their company is responding to these changes. Even if the news is good, the point is the same: Job security is history. American businesses have to increase productivity to remain competitive in the global economy, and American workers have to learn new skills and develop new habits to keep pace.

Managers also have to change. Whereas their competence was once based on controlling techniques and production results, they now have to rely more on attitudes, values, and increasingly creative ways to solve problems. They also have to learn to act fast. Or teach their teams to act fast. Because change has become the norm, today's best managers have become change leaders. They've created decision-making teams that can react quickly, intelligently, and effectively. These teams do best when the team members are empowered with all the skills their managers mastered to become team leaders. In short, the best managers have made their present job descriptions obsolete and have gone on to create new roles to meet the challenges that have yet to be anticipated. People have computers on their desks today with capabilities that 20 years ago cost $5 million and took up the entire floor of a building. What will they have 10 years from now?

Stage 2: Conscious Incompetence

This is the start-up stage for working as a team. The team members know they have to change old habits and learn new skills (technical and behavioral) to remain competitive in the world market. And they're looking to you to show them how. The better the job you do during this stage, the more easily you will solve the problems that await you.

Your job in the conscious incompetence stage is that of the traditional manager: teaching new skills to your subordinates. You tell them what to do and they do it. But be careful: Your team members are also looking to you as a model for how to act on a team. Although you are their leader, you have to start sowing the seeds for your role as a team player.

At the employees' first meeting as a team, you need to establish the ground rules for how the members should behave. With your guidance, the members should together create, establish, and abide by their own codes of behavior. What rules they create are not so important as the ideas they represent: honesty, trust, confidence, fair play, responsibility, and a share in any glory the team achieves.

But there are also some standards you will impose. Every team meeting, for example, will have an agenda to be distributed at least 48 hours and no more than a week before the meeting is scheduled to begin. The team meeting will begin on time (to be fair to those who are punctual) and end on time (because people have other things to do).

Everyone will be expected to participate. This point is crucial. If you have seven members on a team and only four speak up, those four will be making decisions that the other three will have to live by. Stress the importance of everyone contributing and use your position as the team's leader to encourage everyone to participate.

> Ensure that everyone participates at least once on every issue, especially at the early team meetings. Call on any who haven't expressed an opinion before moving on to a new issue. A simple "Mary, what do you think of this proposal?" should do the trick.

Before you have everyone talking at once, however, you'll want to establish some conversational courtesies for the team members to follow:

No such thing as a stupid question. Stupid questions and dumb ideas don't exist. All comments have to be taken seriously by every member of the team.

No negative comments allowed. Anyone who has ever played on a organized sports team knows the value of this one. Members of sports teams obey a code that forbids them to criticize or in any way diminish a teammate. Although they may feel like saying "You idiot! Can't you hold on to the ball!" they have to say, "Don't worry. We'll get them next time."

What works for sports teams also works for other kinds of teams. Allowing and encouraging only positive comments keep everyone's spirits up and each person feels as if the team is behind him or her.

Only questions of clarification. Some teams have a policy that the only questions allowed at any meeting are questions of clarification. Some teams adhere to this policy at meetings where a proposal is being introduced or whenever a suggestion is made.

Permit the "subject challenge." The "subject challenge" is an effective technique for containing digression but should be used only if your team members are mature enough not to abuse it.

Anytime anyone is speaking, any team member has the right to announce a "subject challenge." When the speaker hears the words "subject challenge," that speaker has 30 seconds to justify her point.

Elect a gatekeeper. The gatekeeper's job is to keep the meeting on track. The gatekeeper has the right to interrupt anyone who digresses from the meeting's agenda. If the team agrees the issue is important, it is placed on the next meeting's agenda.

Although the gatekeeper may be appointed or elected, the best functioning teams rotate the position from one meeting to the next. This policy comes with the added feature of giving the quieter team members the opportunity, responsibility, and authority to speak. As the team matures, you'll want to revolve the leadership of the meetings as well.

Summarize. Summarizing the key points, rephrasing in your own words the comments that lead the team in the direction you want it to go, and testing for a consensus all effectively contain digression, manage time, and keep the team members focused on the agenda.

Team meetings can include progress reviews, reports on individual projects, announcements of upcoming events, assignments for follow-up work, agendas for future meetings, and more. But you can be sure your meeting is a success (see pp. 101–105) if it meets these criteria: the meeting starts and ends on time (ends early is even better), the team members feel there was some quality in the work done (the meeting wasn't a waste of time), something was accomplished, and the team members are responsible for following through on any tasks that have to be begun, continued, or completed before the next team meeting.

An early first task for many teams and one that gives the team members an opportunity to practice the behavior codes they're learning is to develop a team mission statement. An easy, low-risk task, the mission statement is the reason for the team's existence, its point of reference for the decisions it makes, the goal it's trying to reach, and the criteria for which it evaluates itself.

A mission statement can be as short as Radisson Hotel's "Yes I Can!" (short statements can be reproduced on buttons, stationery, banners, etc.), or it can be longer (Johnson & Johnson's is four pages).

To help your team members come up with their mission statement, distribute these questions to them prior to the mission-statement meeting. Consider asking for written responses (that will force them to think longer and more seriously):

- What's the purpose of this company?
- How can the team help the company satisfy its purpose?
- What's this company's main product or service?
- Who benefits from this product or service? In what ways?

A final point about the mission statement: Make it real by writing it down and making enough copies of it so everyone on the team cannot help but see it frequently. Anytime the team has to make a decision, it should be able to consult the mission statement to determine if its action is in line with its purpose.

Stage 3: Conscious Competence

This is the stage where your team members have learned the skills you've taught them, but the skills have not yet become a habit or part of their natural behavior. In other words, they feel self-consious and awkward whenever they behave according to the new codes they've adopted.

To reach even this tentative stage, however, is going to challenge all your personal resources. The Conscious Competence stage is the time of confusion, resistance, and conflict.

The previous stages pose little trouble for you because the team members are learning from you as their teacher and you're still retaining most of your power as their leader. Your team members want to know how a team works and how they should behave and you tell them. After hearing about all the wonderful things they're going to accomplish and all the fun they're going to have doing it, the members develop certain expectations. But as they make their way from the conscious incompetent stage to the conscious competent stage, the reality they experience falls short of the expectations they were led to believe. People who for years never listened or spoke at any meetings are now saying what's been on their minds. And a lot of it isn't very pleasant to hear. Especially if these thoughts are accompanied with any pent-up anger, frustration, resentment, or hostility. You told them they had to contribute; now you and everybody else are going to have to listen.

Be patient, listen actively (see pp. 81–85), repeat the codes of behavior each team member is expected to follow and, whenever possible, make every problem a group issue. If a member challenges you directly (e.g, "You got us into this mess!"), ask the person to describe the "mess" and then ask the team if any of its members would like to respond. If there are seven members, at least two of them will be able to say what you would say and, coming from the challenger's peers, the impact will be much greater.

When asking the team members to provide feedback for one another, remember to have them focus on the issue or the behavior and not anyone's personality. Remind them to be specific in their criticism (positive and negative) and ask them to put themselves in the other person's place before speaking. In other words, encourage the team members to do unto others as they would have others do unto them.

When analyzing any conflict among the team members, focus first on defining the problem. If you can accurately define the problem, finding a solution won't be that difficult. More often than not, what you need to resolve the problem is in the conflict itself.

After working with your team members to define the conflict, discuss its causes and what can be done to correct them. Try to find areas where you can agree: What does the team want to accomplish? What results can we expect? Once your team members have defined the problem, your job is to teach them techniques for solving it.

Here are five steps to consider:

1. *Define the problem.* Be flexible. As you gather information, your perception of the problem might change and you will want to redefine it.

2. *Gather information.* As facts and opinions are analyzed, see if the problem has been accurately defined or needs to be restated in another way.

3. *Brainstorm solutions.* Cluster (see pp. 32–35) any and all ideas on an overhead projector or some place else where the team can see all its thoughts at once. Don't eliminate any thoughts or propose any solutions of your own during the brainstorming process. Once all the thoughts of all the team members are recorded, the members should screen, discuss, eliminate, and choose from the ideas.

   During this process, encourage the members to contribute from their experience and be open to all views. And don't arbitrarily overrule any team member. Search instead for a consensus by encouraging all to speak, emphasizing the positives, explaining the seriousness of the negatives, discussing the benefits and problems of any solution, and continually summing up the areas of agreement.

   Important: Think of consensus as a process, not an outcome. A vote is an outcome. Ideas must be heard and understood; discussion is more important than reaching a conclusion.

One of your most important tasks as team leader during the Conscious Competent stage of development is to resist the temptation to step in and solve the team's problems. Encourage the team to consider more than one solution, demonstrate how the safest solution is not always the best solution, coach them — you're no longer their teacher — into developing an action plan. Reinforce the fact that they will be responsible for the decision they make, remove any barriers that might prevent them from acting, and get out of the way. It's their problem, their discussion, their solution, their decision, and their responsibility to implement it.

Reaching the "Conscious Competent" stage, as you might imagine, is the panic stage for the team. Life may not have been great in the traditional power hierarchy, but it was familiar. There were few surprises. And where was all this conflict and airing out of old hostilities getting them? You might find yourself asking the same question when the team members begin challenging you with "Whose idea was this anyhow?" "Who put you in charge of this team?" "What experience do you have running a meeting when all you've done all your life is tell people what to do?"

Again, be patient, read the chapters in this book on how to handle conflict (pp. 153–156) and how to respond to criticism (pp. 162–168), explain that confrontation and resistance to the team process are a part of the normal team-building experience, use the team's mission statement to refocus the members' direction, and keep moving forward.

At some point in the Conscious Competent stage, the team members will ask you to return things to the way they were. Or at least do one thing for them the way you used to. Resist this temptation, which will be difficult because the team members will obviously need you, the task they will ask you to perform will be easy for you and, in light of all the tough times the team has been through, you will want to help them.

Again, make every problem a group issue and thrust the responsibility of solving it back on the team. The truth is that you can't go back to the way things were even if you wanted to. The team members have already experienced a taste of independence and authority they've never known; they've been able to challenge themselves and each other in new ways; they've developed a different way of relating to you; they couldn't give these things up if they wanted to. And neither of you want them too, although neither of you may know that yet.

And as if things weren't bad enough, production has gone down. For this reason, the third stage of the team's development is also the panic stage for upper management. If management steps in at this point, decides the team concept hasn't worked, and pulls the plug on you, consider looking for another job because your life is going to be miserable. You've already given away most of your authority to the team, which the members will not give back to you, and management is in a position to blame you for everything that goes wrong from here on in. Note: It's *crucial* for upper management to realize that production is going to go down before beginning the

team-building process. It's as inevitable a part of the team-building experience as the team members' confrontations. How far down production goes,
how long it stays there, and to what degree the team members continue
bickering with each other depends on how well you've prepared them to
meet the team-building challenges, how successful you are at making the
transition from manager to coach to coordinator or facilitator, and how
much support you're going to get from upper management when push
comes to shove.

Here's what the process looks like visually:

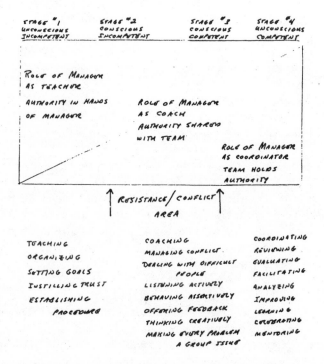

When you're in the early stages of team development (far left-hand side
of the visual), establishing precedents and teaching behavior skills are more
important than any task. During the middle/resistance/conflict period,
your focus is mostly on people. Like a coach, you've given your team its
instructions; now it's the team's turn to perform. Nevertheless, you have to
be there to help the team make its transition to self-management. Along the
way, all your interpersonal resources will be tested as they never have been.

The final stage of development marks the team's successful transition.
No longer a group of people working together, they are now a self-directed

team. You are no longer needed as their teacher and coach. It's time to change your role to that of coordinator/facilitator/mentor.

Stage 4: Unconscious Competence

This is the stage you and your team have been aiming for. The team members have learned to work together with minimal conflict, they've practiced the skills you taught them, they've completed enough projects to have some confidence in the team process, they've raised their production to a level above what it was before the team was formed, and have created projects of their own to work on.

In short, the team is running on synergy, that intangible component where a group of people working as a team can get more work done in less time with better quality results than any similar number of people working as a mere group.

Imagine geese flying in formation for a perfect example of synergy. Why the "V" formation? To cut down on wind resistance. Why the constant honking? To encourage everybody to keep up. The leadership rotates and, if any goose drops out of the formation, two will follow and stay with it until it recovers or can't go on. Studies have shown that geese flying in formation can fly 93 percent farther than any goose flying alone.

In the same way that the geese no longer need a constant leader, neither does the team that reaches the Unconscious Competent stage. But there's no reason for you to panic. As you once changed your role from teacher to coach, now you will again change your role to that of a coordinator/facilitator/mentor. In other words, you now service the team as resource rather than direct it as a leader.

Here's how:

Evaluate. You've been evaluating your team's progress all along, empowering its members with the skills you know, and providing training in the areas where it is needed. But now you may wish to take a more formal approach toward determining what worked and can be repeated and what didn't work and can be learned from. Perhaps you can update job descriptions, create profiles of the team members, determine the technical and behavior skills they will need for future projects, and select those members who could be given the opportunity to help teams that are struggling or form new teams.

Consider empowering the team with the authority to evaluate itself. Ask the team members to create their own criteria and measure themselves as individuals and as a team against the standards they've established. Having the team evaluate itself helps the members become aware of how it achieved certain levels of accomplishment and what it needs to do to reach those levels again. Now the team has the responsibility traditionally held by the leader. They don't want to be told what to do; and they certainly don't need to be told.

In the traditional power hierarchy, managers are very much like parents: they take care of things. The employees are treated like children. In this system, the manager is burdened with responsibility, and the employees are virtually powerless. In the team system, the team members, with their leader acting as a team member, collaborate. They share the planning, implementation, accountability, and rewards of any project. Now the team leader-come-facilitator is responsible for process, not outcome. In fact, you can measure a team's maturity and level of development by how much responsibility it has accepted from the leader. Similarly, you can measure a leader's success by how much authority has been given the team.

Celebrate. This is an important activity at every stage of the team's development. One of the major causes of stress is the lack of closure in our lives. Due in large part to our Puritan work ethic, we often suffer guilt for feeling good about our accomplishments, as if for some reason we deserve to work hard but don't deserve to reward ourselves. Very often, as we near the end of any task, we start looking into the next project on our agenda. Or we do several things at once so that, even though we complete tasks, the remaining tasks take us away from any time we might have to enjoy the satisfaction of having achieved something.

And upper-management doesn't help. Monitoring our individual as well as our team progress, management seems to always feel the need to come up with something for us to do to increase productivity and profit.

One of the most effective services you can provide for you, your company, and your team members is a sense of closure: "We've completed this project; let's enjoy the feeling of a job well done." Go to lunch together, take the afternoon off, have a party.

Empower. Encourage your team to go beyond the end of any project. Make it a leader in its field by developing a vision for your company. Compare your team's work with the most creative organizations in the industry and brainstorm what you can do together to compete with them. Then present your results as strategic issues that require the serious attention of upper management. Or, if upper management has done the job it was supposed to do in helping build the team, inform upper management of your next goal and get to work on reaching it.

Form. Some time after a team reaches the perfect state of synergy, it can become stale. The members get along well enough and efficiently complete their projects, but they're not creating any new approaches to the problems they face, they haven't come up with any proposals for projects they could be working on, and upper management doesn't have anything else for them to do.

This is a good time to consider breaking up the team and dividing its members among other teams or asking them to form new teams of their own.

To create a successful team, you need the right combination of people and technical skills. Whatever technical skills are needed should be determined by the team's project or the reason why it's being formed. The personality make-up of the team, however, is a different story. To create the best team of personalities, you need to identify and combine a balance of Directors, Relators, Thinkers, and Operators (see pp. 148–152).

Form a team with too many Directors and you will have too many people who are unwilling to share beneficial information going off in too many different directions. Because Directors are often competitive, they'll hold on to information that gives them an edge over everyone else. On the other hand, they have no qualms about taking information that will enable them to finish first, stay ahead, and come out on top.

A team of Relators, on the other hand, rarely gets much work done. Its members are so busy trying to win each other's acceptance and approval. They have to make sure everybody gets along with one another before getting down to work.

Teams of Thinkers, unlike Relators, get to work but they never complete anything. They get into the research and are never heard from again because there's always another book to be read, analyzed, weighed, measured, and discussed.

Operators, of course, get things done but nothing that amounts to very much. Follow directions, yes; maintain a system, yes; repeat a behavior, you bet. Brainstorm for a new solution to an old problem? Brainstorm, yes; but come up with something new? Not likely.

A Final Word on Teams

Teams differ from traditional work groups in the sense that their members are interdependent with one another. That's where the synergy comes from. The ideal self-managed team works in a climate of trust. Encouraged by their leader to question, challenge, and explore, they know that conflict is a normal part of the growing process and focus on the goals they have the responsibility and decision-making authority to achieve.

Team leaders differ from traditional managers in that they enable rather than control, focus on process rather than content, are more learners than teachers, and facilitate rather than direct. They get people involved, encourage them to do their best, foster open, honest, and direct communication, act as a resource rather than a judge, as a mentor rather than a boss, reward mutual support and cooperation, and, in general, make work fun without losing their own sense of humor. When your team members recognize the benefits of helping one another, work hard to achieve their goals, stimulate each other to succeed, and discover they don't need a leader, you know you've done your job.

Index

Action:
    definition of, 7
    as discipline, 35
    identifying problems with, 13
    maintaining focus on, 13
    as time management, 23
    versus wrong action, 7
    visualizing, 13
    as a way to say "no," 25
Appraisals:
    by others, 176-177
    of others, 175-176
    of projects, 35-36
Assertion:
    during confrontations, 121-123
    to increase in self, 120-121
    with respect for others, 120
    as a state of mind, 119-120
Attitude:
    for creativity, 138
    for criticism, 162-163
    definition of, 6
    developing the right, 4-6, 34
    for leadership, 146
    for listening, 82-83
    for stress, 113-114

Burnout, preventing on the job, 125-126

Career, balancing with family, 135-140
Change:
    fear of, 9
    implementing, 9-10
    in vocabulary, 36
"Clustering":
    as a creativity technique, 128-129
    as a memory technique, 78
    as a planning technique, 32-34
    as a presentation technique, 95-96

as a writing technique, 63-64
Comparison with others, 5
Conflict:
    defining the problem, 156
    monitoring a resolution, 155-156
    as an opportunity for growth, 154-155
    preparing for, 153-154
Cover letters for job applications, 50-53
Creativity:
    right attitude for, 128
    right side vs. left side brain techniques, 127
    techniques for, 128-129
Criticism:
    attitude toward, 162-163
    of others, 165-168
    responding to, 163-165

Deadlines:
    establishing, 12
    importance of, 12
    as a way to manage time, 25
Delegating:
    as time management, 26
    deciding what to, 159
    knowing when to, 158
    to ensure success, 159-161
Difficult People:
    "directors," 149-150
    "operators," 151-152
    relating to, 152-153
    "relators," 150
    "thinkers," 152
    types of, 149-153
Discipline:
    as action, 35
    definition of, 15
    developing, 15

Family:
    arranging child care, 136-138
    balancing with career, 135-136
    combating guilt, 139-140
    creating time, 139
    getting household help, 138-139
Fear:
    of change, 9
    combating, 6, 9-10
    handling, 6
Files:
    accordion, use of, 30
    for achievements, 31
    arranging, 17
    consolidating, 17
    eliminating, 17
Firing people:
    how to, 179-180
Flexibility:
    to avoid ruts, 10
    to create goals, 14
Focus:
    for acting, 13
    for controlling, 7
    for getting started, 15
    for maintaining, 13
    on one thing at a time, 25
    on the present, 15
    on what's important, 31

Goals:
    characteristics of, 11-12
    importance of, 16-17
    flexibility, 14

Hiring people, how to, 179-181

Interruptions, how to reduce, 26-27
Interviews:
    during, 57-59
    following, 60
    illegal questions, 58-59
    preparing for, 55-56

Jobs:
    combating burnout at, 124-126
    creating resumes for, 43-49
    interviewing for, 54-60
    searching for, 41-42
    writing cover letters for, 50-53

Leadership:
    characteristics of, 146-147
    theories of, 144-146
Letters:
    format for, 70-71
    for job applications, 50-53
    postscripts for, 71
    preparing to write, 68, 72-73
    proofreading, 65-67
Listening:
    to determine what's important, 83-84
    to hear more effectively, 81-83
    to reply after, 84-85
Lists:
    to avoid procrastination, 19
    to manage time, 23
    as a way to organize, 16

Maslow, Abraham, 169
McClelland, David, 173-174
Meetings:
    after, 104
    creating ideas for, 104-105
    establishing eye-contact at, 97-98
    fielding questions at, 99-100
    as interruptions, 29
    leading, 102
    opening, 96-97
    participating at, 103
    preparing for, 94
    reviewing, 103-104
    visual aids at, 98
Memory:
    to remember more, 77-80.
Memos:
    format for, 70
    proofreading, 65-67
    before writing, 68, 72-73
Motivation:
    to achieve for self, 14
    with behavior, 14
    to increase production in others, 170-173
    to maintain for self, 14
    theories of, 173-177
    what workers want, 169-170

Negotiation to reach win-win-solutions,
    106-109

Organization:
    accordion files, 30
    of goals, 16
    of tasks, 31
    of lists, 16
    of work area, 17-18

Paperwork, reducing, 30
Past, dealing with, 4
Perfectionism:
    as a cause of procrastination, 21
    how to overcome, 21
Plans:
    how to create, 13
    how to implement plans, 13-15
    to manage time, 23
    for projects, 32-34
    for the work day, 24
Positive Thinking:
    importance of, 10
    in vocabulary, 37
Presentations:
    establishing eye-contact at, 97-98
    fielding questions at, 99-100
    openings, 96-97
    preparing for, 94
    visual aids for, 98
Procrastination:
    accepting, 19
    avoiding, 19-21
    perfectionism as a cause of, 21
Projects:
    acting on, 34-35
    "clustering," 33
    planning, 32-34
    reviewing, 35-36
Proofreading of memos and letters, 65-67

Reading:
    for comprehension, 77-80
    for speed, 74-77
Resumes for job applications, 43-49
Reviews:
    by others, 176-177
    of others, 175-176

    of projects, 35-36
Rewards:
    for accomplishments, 5,14
    importance of, 5,6,14,17, 25
    visualizing, 14
Risks:
    conflict with, 130
    taking, 131-132

"Salami Technique:"
    to avoid procrastination, 20
    definition of, 20
Selling on the telephone, 92-94
Sexual harassment:
    general guidelines for avoiding, 133
    responding to, 134
Speaking:
    after listening, 84-85
    in public, 94-100
Stress:
    preventing, 113-115
    responding to, 115-118
    two kinds of, 113

Team Building:
    advantages of, 184
    four stages of development, 184-195
    as opposed to work groups, 195-196
    reasons for, 183-184
Telemarketing, 92-94
Telephone:
    calling, 88-90
    customer service calls, 90-91
    sales calls, 92-94
    screening, 90
    when answering, 87-88
Time:
    analyzing use of, 22
    establishing deadlines, 12
    making use of at meetings, 30
    making use of free, 6
    management of, 23-31
    planning use of, 23

Visual Aids for presentations, 98
Visualization:
    of goals, 10, 13-14
    imagining the ideal you, 4

Visualization (*Continued*)
  of rewards, 14
  for successful outcomes, 10
Vocabulary:
  positive words, 37
  unintended meanings, 38-39

Win-Win Solutions, 106-107

Work area:
  organizing, 17-18
  reducing interruptions in, 26
Writing
  correcting, 65-67
  creating ideas for, 63-65
  "freewriting," 65
  three step process, 63-67

About the Author

Richard Andersen is president of On the Job, Inc.., a management training and communications consulting company. With clients such as TRW, IBM, and the Internal Revenue Service, he has worked with senior-level administrators in every field of business and industry. Dr. Andersen is also a popular seminar leader who has taught thousands of business professionals what the best management systems have to offer. He is the author of 13 books, including the top-selling *Writing That Works* (McGraw-Hill). Dr. Andersen lives in Amherst, Massachusetts.